T0147976

Laughin'
ON THE ITHER SIDE
o'ma face

A L L A N   D O D D S

authorHOUSE®

AuthorHouse™
1663 Liberty Drive
Bloomington, IN 47403
www.authorhouse.com
Phone: 1-800-839-8640

Published by AuthorHouse   06/22/2012

ISBN: 978-1-4685-0502-3 (sc)
ISBN: 978-1-4685-0503-0 (hc)
ISBN: 978-1-4685-0501-6 (e)

CONTENTS

DEDICATION

This book is dedicated to the memory of my Mother Cecilia Dodds (1911-2006) and my Father Gilbert Dodds (1905-1976), without whom this book could not have been written.

It is also written in fond memory of two great friends, Jack Galbraith and Keith Burrows, without whom my life would have been a lot less fun.

ACKNOWLEDGMENTS

The Author wishes to thank the following for their assistance in the production of this book:

Peter Stubbs, for reawakening an exile's interest in Edinburgh's past through his website;

Ian Nicol for making helpful suggestions about cover design and narrative style;

Nigel Baxter for allowing me to reproduce the photo of Broughton Place Church members;

The Scottish National Portrait Gallery for permitting me to reproduce the cover picture by Alexander (Sandy) Moffat:

'Poets'Pub'(Norman MacCaig, Sorley MacLean, Hugh MacDiarmid, Iain Crichton Smith, George Mackay Brown, Sidney Goodsir Smith, Edwin Morgan, Robert Garioch, Alan Bold and John A. Tonge).

The Author wishes to accept that, if any of the individuals depicted in this book should, upon reading it, feel unfairly portrayed, he readily concedes that memories of past events are by their nature subjective, and not necessarily shared by others who may have experienced those same events.

CHAPTER 1

THE WAR YEARS

According to my Birth Certificate I was born in a private clinic in Palmerstone Place on May 23rd, 1943. When the Consultant Obstetrician learned that my Father was a low earning Insurance Clerk currently fighting in Germany for our freedom he waived his fee. Much later I was to find out that on the day before, 2,000 tons of British bombs had been dropped on Dortmund. On the following day, my first day on earth, a further 2,000 tons of bombs and incendiaries were dropped on Dusseldorf. Later in that week, Essen was bombed, followed by Hamburg. In Europe, more newborn babies such as myself would have perished than survived. But of course, as an infant, I was blissfully unaware of such a backdrop to my new existence, although I was gradually to become aware of the deprivations and dangers faced daily by those around us in our tenement block in Howard Street, Canonmills, where I grew up to become an Edinburgh lad.

In those days the Canonmills area was a much less genteel place than it is today as there was still a fair amount of industrial activity there: Morrison and Gibbs and the Scottish Daily Mail works; a whisky bond; an ice factory in Canon Street and McGlashen's, monumental masons. All through the night I would listen to the sound of the huge beam saw rasping back and forth over a block of granite on which the following morning stonemasons would carve the name of some Edinburgh dignitary, before transporting it by horse and cart along the road by the Water of Leith to Warriston Cemetery where it may still stand. These industries provided a bustling and noisy accompaniment to everyday life and their familiar sounds were comforting to an infant, even although my parents would complain about them from time to time.

Just along the road, Canon Street was notorious as a slum, with scruffy children sporting 'candles' from their noses regularly roaming the streets. Candles was the term my Mother used for the thick strings of yellow mucus that would descend from their nostrils, only to disappear rapidly at a sniff, then gradually but inevitably reassert themselves a few moments later. Low grade upper respiratory infections were endemic and most of us lived our lives in fear of even greater threats to our health such as scarlet fever, diphtheria or, Heaven forefend, polio. Gangs of working class children would maraud as far as Warriston Crescent where they would invariably be met with hostility from the posher kids who did not fear to take them on. We knew these gangs as 'The Baddies', and a watchful eye had to be maintained in order to keep a safe distance from their aggressive tendencies.

Canon Street had its moments for a child, and when the baddies were off on the prowl somewhere else we would feel safe to go up the street on our way to the play park in Eyre Place where such delights as swings, a chute, a merry-go-round and a 'cheese-cutter' awaited. About halfway up the street on the left hand side was the ice factory. In the summer, on our way past, we would pick up huge chunks of ice from the cobbled street and suck them until they vanished, our mouths numbed into submission. Those crystalline jewels were works of art to a child's eye; clear, smooth sculptures infused with delicate tubes of air trapped within. As refreshing as an ice cream, beautiful to behold and, above all, free at the point of collection.

At the other end of the temperature scale were the Guy Fawkes' night bonfires that took place every year. For about two weeks before the Fifth, piles of wooden pallets, old furniture and anything that would burn would begin to appear right in the middle of the road at the foot of the hill, blocking access to all traffic. The authorities evidently saw no harm in this, and the Police were never called to intervene to restore passage to vehicles. One year, the heat from the bonfire was so intense that it caused the paint from a nearby shopkeeper's door to blister quite severely, but again, no one called the Fire Brigade. Such behaviour now would not be tolerated, but we took such freedoms quite for granted then.

When I was an infant, Mother soon became a familiar figure to me, whereas by contrast Father was a barely known visitor who occasionally dropped in on us quite unannounced, and whose identity only gradually became clear to me. My first memory of him was when I was still very young, probably about six months of age. As I recall, he was quite unlike anyone I had ever seen. He wore a khaki battledress and sported a bristling Hitler-like toothbrush moustache that reeked of cigarette smoke. Whether or not this choice of facial ornamentation was a deliberate act of parody on his behalf I shall never know, but he retained it throughout his life. Father was not skilled in handling an infant, and when he balanced me on his knee I genuinely feared that I would overbalance onto the floor: hardly inspiring confidence in him.

Almost as soon as he had settled himself in with Mother and myself (the former rather more than the latter), Father would be off again, his soldier's boots clickety-clacking up Brandon Terrace as he headed for the Waverley Station, until the sound died away, to be replaced by Mother's barely stifled weeping. Not that I was upset myself, to tell the truth. In fact on the contrary, because it meant that 'normal' life could now resume, by way of enjoying Mother's undivided attention and being indulged, as opposed to being left alone crying in the box room at Father's insistence of a 'proper' night with Mother, which meant 'noises off' for me.

Mother was an anxious parent, having been widowed after just two years of a previous, only too brief marriage. Her first husband Jack had suffered from congenital heart disease, but in spite of this knowledge she had bravely married him. When he inevitably died, Mother was left with the ownership of a second floor flat in Howard Street. Father had met her before the War and obviously thought that she was a good catch: an attractive young widow with property in a reasonably respectable district of the city They married in 1940 and the very next year Gibbie, as he was known rather than the formal 'Gilbert', was called up to train for Army service in strife-torn Europe.

Army training meant Father having to leave Edinburgh to travel to barracks at Catterick. I believe that his regiment, the Royal Corps of Signals of the 15th Scottish Division, had to march all the way from Edinburgh to Yorkshire. Army leave was intermittent and short-lived. A posting to West Malling soon followed, and Mother later confided to me that on one occasion she took the train there to spent a few brief hours with him on one of his twenty-four hour passes. I was thus conceived there in an apple orchard, which I find quite romantic. Father was not impressed by my impending arrival: indeed, for many years he doubted that one fleeting moment of passion could have resulted in a pregnancy.

Our next-door neighbour at Number Seven, Mr Murdoch, who enjoyed a protected job as a Pharmacist in Civvy Street, became the prime suspect, and relationships on the stair landing were always frosty between us for many years post-war. It was really only when I became a teenager and came to resemble my Father physically that he reluctantly conceded that I was more than likely his son rather than Mr Murdoch's. The photo overleaf shows Father in his battle dress at home on leave before he gained his Sergeant's stripes.

As an infant, my first memories were of significant events and local places. With the Royal Botanic Garden only five minutes' walk away, Mother spent much time there with me in my high pram in a vain attempt to stop me from crying, of which I apparently did quite a lot, hoping that I would drop off to sleep. Instead, I took an animated interest in everything I saw and devoured all experiences avidly. One of my earliest memories is of seeing snow for the first time in my life. In retrospect, this must have been around the beginning of December when I was six months old. Instead of the muddy paths and sodden green grass surrounding them, a smooth blanket of freshly fallen snow enveloped the whole landscape, knitting it together in a new and, to my eyes, quite beautiful and seamless fashion.

The pale sun that day cast soft shadows on the undulating surfaces and, looking over the side of my pram, I watched transfixed as

Mother ruffled the smooth surface of the snow with a long twig. I was mesmerised, although I cannot articulate anything more about my feelings or thoughts, if indeed infants have thoughts at the age of six months. I do, however, recall the awe in which I held my Mother for her power to wreak such a transformation on the world with such little effort. Many decades later, talking to her in her latter years, she was able to inform me of the reliability of that recollection, adding that she had in fact written my name in the snow, although the squiggles meant nothing to me then other than a demonstration of her ineffable wisdom and infinite power. The photo below shows me in my Moses' basket just two months before I formed that first and lasting recollection.

Many of my earliest memories are of sitting in my high pram during the first winter of my life. The taste of wet woollen mittens remains vividly with me, and my Mother later confirmed that I used to chew them incessantly. So much so that she had to put mustard on my fingers as a deterrent as I had chewed through the mittens to the skin beneath. Strangely, although I cannot recall the pain of skinned fingers, or the taste of mustard, I cannot stand its taste as an adult, so some unconscious memory must be there. Not so with the memory of the air-raid siren going of at the Police box on Canonmills Bridge. One day it began wailing just as we were passing it and that set me off screaming. The Police box can still be seen there today, minus the siren, and unlike then, its current existence serves no purpose other than as a silent witness to a long-forgotten conflict.

As I developed, other adults would soon become familiar to me when relatives began to appear on the scene. The first I was told to call 'Nana', which I found confusing as Mother called her Amie. To complicate matters even more, her Christian name was Christina. Nana was an elderly woman whom I later learned was Mother's own Mother, although no one had wished to explain this to me when she was alive. Mother referred to Nana as her 'Aunt', for reasons that again did not become clear to me until after her death. Apparently, Nana had borne my Mother out of wedlock and no one other than her knew the identity of the father. It later emerged that he had been a musician and instrument maker living in London, but the mystery remained as to his personal identity.

In her youth Nana had left Edinburgh to seek her fame and fortune in London, taking up the post of Governess to a well-to-do family, during which time she had become pregnant and had then been summarily dismissed, as was the custom in those days. Indeed, Nana could have found herself committed to an institution on the grounds of 'moral imbecility', as many such as her were before World War 2. Returning to Edinburgh in disgrace, Nana's family responded by selling up their fashionable flat in Great King Street and moving to Musselburgh where Nana was set up as proprietor of a tearoom. The pretence was contrived that Nana was Mother's Aunt and that Mother had been an adopted orphan: a pretence that was to outlive Nana.

Regrettably, Mother never found out who her father was, only that she had been christened Cecilia after the name of a violin that he had been making at the time of her conception, and Nana took his identity with her to the grave. The photo below shows Father, Mother and Nana on a summer's day out.

When I was in my high pram Mother and I used to visit Nana almost daily at her tiny sweetie shop in Pitt Street, now demolished with the street later being incorporated into Dundas Street. Nana lived in the 'back shop', which consisted of a small room with a bed, a range and a water closet the size of a cupboard. Next door on the South side was Irvine Electrical where owners of radios could take their accumulators to be recharged. On the North side was Barry Brown, Tailor; Miss McCullough, Tobacconist; Miss Stewart, Haberdasher, and McVittie & Guest, Bakers. Across the road was Stewart's Bar (still there today in remarkably unchanged form) and Mr Moran's Italian ice-cream shop. Just around the opposite corner in Henderson Row was Mr McArthur, the Dentist, a man with whom I was to have repeated and painful encounters over the years.

The photograph below shows where Nana's shop was until the row of properties was demolished around the early 1960s, to be replaced by modern buildings that don't really add character to the street. The photograph was taken by J Campbell Harper, Photographers, who were based further up the hill at Number Ten Dundas Street. The neatly dressed woman standing at the bus stop is Anne Harper, daughter of the Managing Director. Unbeknown to me then, I was later to have association with J Campbell Harper.

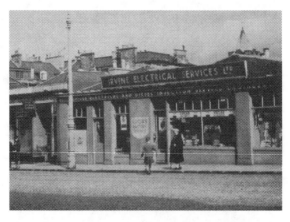

Those familiar landmarks provided a stable structure to my early years and I have many memories of that part of Edinburgh dating from the age of between one and five years. Among them was living through the blackout with the air-raid siren periodically sounding: a signal to leave the flat and go downstairs to the communal air-raid shelter that was located in the 'back green'. For reasons best known to herself, Mother never availed herself of this facility and instead simply went about her normal business of cooking, washing, dusting, rearranging the furniture, and generally pretending that everything was all right. One night a Warden rang the doorbell to warn us that our window was showing a light and Mother was ordered to rearrange the blackout curtains on pain of dire consequences.

Sleep for me, as an infant was never really part of my agenda, for reasons not initially identified. I distinctly remember lying in my cot during the night listening to the comforting sound of Mother's breathing in the bed nearby. Unknown to me, Mother was also lying wide-awake listening to the comforting sounds of my breathing, and between us, we managed to keep each another needlessly awake. Consultations with the then experts in child development produced the recommendation that I be left in a room on my own. After a whole night of undisturbed sleep, Mother was relieved to find me alive and well in the morning without her need to monitor my every breath. It is only with hindsight and the childhood memories still fresh in my mind that I can now understand the cause of the problem: mutual anxiety!

Never really trusting her own instincts, Mother frequently sought professional advice on child rearing. After all, she was living as a single parent without any previous experience of infants, and being of a naturally anxious disposition she always feared the worst when some new behaviour manifested itself. In her latter years she recounted to me an incident when she had noticed that my head lolled about when unsupported. Panicking that some developmental disorder was making itself manifest, she immediately called good old Doctor Thorpe, the family physician who, when asked if the infant was showing signs of mental defectiveness, retorted, "Not the child, the Mother!" Professionals could confidently speak their minds in those days without running the risk of incurring litigation instigated by the offended recipient of their unwelcomed wisdom.

Doctor Thorpe became a familiar figure in our household, partly on account of Mother's ongoing anxieties and partly because I was somewhat sickly myself. Croup was a regular affliction that always brought a swift response from Dr Thorpe who had an uncanny instinct for a genuine problem as opposed to an imaginary one. I have lost count of the number of times he sat by my bedside in the small hours, waiting for an emetic to take effect and clear the phlegm from my constricted windpipe, enabling me to breathe again and allowing my blue lips to return to a healthier pink. Sometimes my temperature would rise so high that I would begin to hallucinate, and I distinctly remember seeing sailors dancing a jig on the chimney pots on the flats opposite. On one occasion, struggling vainly for breath, I informed Mother that I was going to die, and I remember no fear being attached to this belief. Thanks to Dr Thorpe, my life was literally saved on more than one occasion by his assiduous ministrations for which my parents had to pay hard-earned money as the National Health Service did not come into being until 1948 by the time that I had reached the age of five.

On a normal night in wartime when the air-raid sirens were moaning, I would listen to the throbbing of the engines of German bombers as they passed overhead on their way to attack the Rosyth shipyards, attempts that were thankfully thwarted by our naval defences in the Firth of Forth. In the winter months those sounds would be accompanied by the sonorous booming of the foghorns far out to sea. Whereas I looked forward to listening nightly to the sounds of aeroplane engines, air-raid sirens and fog-horns, their effect on Mother was evidently not so reassuring, and her anxieties were communicated to me as much by body language as speech, which of course was initially incomprehensible.

The first developmental milestone that I vividly recall achieving was that of teething, at around six months of age. It was a rather painful process, with inflamed gums that throbbed. Mother's initial remedy was to give me a Farley's Rusk to chew on, but they were vile, rough and quite intolerable. So Mother purchased a teething ring, a pink plastic affair no doubt containing highly toxic ingredients by modern standards. I found this quite pleasant and recall the feeling of relief when a new tooth emerged through aching gums. After a week or two the teething ring had been somewhat reduced in size and bore distinct bite marks, whereupon it disappeared as magically as it had materialised. I could now bite and chew more solid food, such as was available that is with the rationing that was then enforced.

As the months passed, and with my first birthday looming, I distinctly recall speaking my first words. Those words do not appear in any academic textbook on childhood development, and it is to my Mother that I owe their unique utterance. Part of growing up involved becoming dry at night and towards the end of my first year I perceived that being dry was a Mother-set target that I strove hard to meet. After a few successes, Mother was so pleased that she effectively left my nappy off altogether at night. However, my skills in that department were not altogether reliable, and when the occasional accident did occur, Mother, on entering my bedroom and sensing from the unmistakable odour that all was not well, would exclaim: "My little ammonia boy!" This was said in a kindly fashion, but the word 'ammonia' was fascinating to me. When another little accident happened one night, I anticipated Mother's comment in the morning and before she could open her mouth I proudly declared: "Monia boy!" Mother beamed. I was one year old and felt very pleased with myself at being able to speak.

After that, I realised that everything had a name and I would point to various things that caught my attention, asking: "What dat?" Mother was always able to help me out and my vocabulary grew apace. However, sometimes I preferred my own words for things as the words that Mother gave me sometimes sounded unpleasant. A good example of this is when I was just over a year old and Mother took me to the Botanics just as the trees were coming into bloom. Seeing the blossom for the first time I naturally pointed to it, asking what it was called. Mother's word 'blossom' sounded too like the word 'bottom', which I knew to be a bad word, so I insisted for many weeks on calling blossom 'blossman', a much nicer-sounding word in my view, for what it was worth. The photo below shows me on my first birthday.

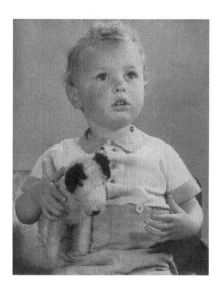

At around the same time as I began to be out of nappies and started talking, I recall taking my first independent steps. It was morning and Mother was doing the vacuuming. In order to get out of her way I got up and teetered from one chair to another, a distance of only a few feet. Mother immediately stopped what she was doing and picked up the telephone, animatedly informing the recipient of the call that I had begun to walk unaided. I overheard a male voice at the other end and assumed that she was speaking to my Father. The voice turned out, I was later told, to be that of my Grandfather: Father was many hundreds of miles away in Germany fighting in a war I knew absolutely nothing about and whose outward signs were of complete normality, but the mistaken inference was understandable as I had overheard a gruff, male voice speaking at the other end.

Being able to walk meant that there was no further need for a pram, and I graduated to pushchair mobility for extended excursions. Shopping trips were always memorable because the occurrence of some minor disaster by Mother's standards, or some really bizarre event by my own, could be guaranteed to happen. Regular visits to Stockbridge were made as the few local Canonmills shops had little to offer during wartime rationing. Meat, such as could be obtained, was purchased at Gavin Nimmo's shop in Henderson Row, now a private dwelling house, even although we lived immediately next door to Porteous the Butchers in Howard Street. Mr Nimmo was reputed by Mother to be fond of the drink, and his purple nose confirmed her suspicions without the need for any independent evidence or indeed professional opinion.

The sight of Mr Nimmo's nose invariably filled me with nervous apprehension. In the cold winter months it would spontaneously produce a drip whose length seemed to defy the laws of physics as I had then deduced them. I remember watching in anticipation as the drip eventually broke free of its host, landing fair and square on the piece of mutton that he was preparing with his customary concerns for hygiene. Mother, typically fastidious about such matters, pretended not to notice, and in spite of her habitual forthrightness, the offender was spared her disapprobation. Falling out with Gavin Nimmo would have meant no decent meat for us of any sort, not even offal such as tripe, liver, sweetbreads or kidneys which were regular fare in wartime and which I grew to detest.

Not so with Mr Murray, the Grocer and Wine Merchant at Number 1 Howard Street, now an Italian restaurant. Mr Murray was reputed to live in a posh house, which I have established by my research to have been a modest villa flat in Warriston Gardens. I did not then understand that 'posh' is a purely relative term, or that we ourselves were placed socially just one barely comfortable rung above the slum-dwellers in Canon Street. Mr Murray was noted for his economies, both in terms of chitchat to his customers and his consumption of energy. To a toddler, his shop presented itself as a vast emporium of beckoning comestibles: brown sacks containing potatoes, carrots, turnips and other unidentifiable vegetables, such as could be obtained in wartime. Whilst his sister attended to customers at the front shop, Mr Murray preferred to lurk in the back, observing them from a safe distance and no doubt privately passing judgment on their buying habits, dress taste and morals.

Mother would constantly complain about how uncharitable and inhospitable Mr Murray was, and moreover how cold and damp his shop presented itself, being only barely warmed by a small gas fire with three porcelain elements. One day, whilst Mother was chatting to Mr Murray's sister, I happened upon a carrot lying on the floor that I decided would benefit from toasting on the gas fire. Mother had apparently just wise-cracked about how pleased she was to see the 'central heating' on, whereupon there was a sort of a breaking noise, followed by an instant and irreversible malfunction of the gas fire. I reviewed my handiwork, but not with the same eyes as did Mr Murray, whose immediate appearance from behind the scenes occasioned some awkward back-pedalling by Mother who faithfully promised to replace the broken parts at no expense to The Proprietor. To no avail, I have to relate: in wartime no such spares were available and by the time the War ended the appliance was deemed obsolescent. We never set foot in Mr Murray's shop again, such was the shame of it.

Tenement life was interesting for a child because people would come and go in the course of their lives and business. The Postman would often ring the doorbell to hand over the infrequent mail in person, and at Christmas Mother would reward him with a glass of sherry when he delivered Christmas cards. The Coalman was another regular guest who would appear bearing dirty bulging sacks, which would be shouldered through the hall and into the coal-cupboard off the living room. Mother would prepare herself for this onslaught by putting down newspapers all the way along the hall floor from the front door. But somehow the coalman always managed to scuff the corner of the bag on the cream-coloured distempered wall, leaving lasting evidence of his visit. Mother would then have to telephone Grandpa to glean from him some reliable remedy. And the mess that the chimney sweep left behind him invariably sent Mother into paroxysms of anxiety, especially when he had not been ordered and a brush would descend unexpectedly down our chimney instead of the one it was destined for. After that two chimney sweeps would arrive, one calling "Weep" up the chimney, the other listening at the row of pots on the roof above to ensure that no similar mistakes were made.

Another highlight of the day would be when a card would mysteriously appear hanging on the polished brass handle of the front door bearing the injunction: "Your Turn on the Common Stair and Landing". This referred not so much to a musical or dramatic event, but rather to the more prosaic fact that it was our turn to pay the 'stair lady'. Even more alarming was the card bearing the sinister words: "Your Turn on the Back Passage." I don't believe that this referred to the use of suppositories. Mother never referred to the stair ladies by their proper names, as I was to discover to my cost. The first woman I remember, who lived in a slum in Canon Street, would ring the doorbell at 6.30am requesting a bucket of hot water, a cloth and a scrubbing brush. Mother was always ready on such mornings with the range already blazing and a black kettle on the boil, and I was invariably awakened by those early morning activities.

One day I asked Mother what the woman's name was. "Dean Swift", she replied with her usual cutting wit referring, as I later found out, to the speed at which the work was carried out. The next time the woman rang the bell I was awake and ready to be first to answer the door. Mother called out to me from within the house, asking who it was. "Mrs Swift", I confidently piped. Later, Mrs Swift was to be replaced by another anonymous person whom Mother had instinctively identified as an alcohol abuser. Once again, I had the opportunity of conveying Mother's uninvited opinion to the hapless recipient when she called one morning. Answering the door ahead of Mother, I heard her voice asking who it was. "The lady who drinks the gin", I reliably informed her. Stair ladies were always difficult to get after that.

Living in a tenement on a main road with a tramway running past it made for excellent free entertainment. Often, the tram's trolley would become detached from the overhead wire and the tram would grind to a halt, resuming its journey only after its conductor had alighted to reattach the trolley amidst an impressive shower of sparks. Once in a while all night entertainment would be available when workmen came to cut out worn tram rails and weld in new ones, or to repair the points which were always wearing out. The whole street would then be lit up with blue flashes and sparks as oxyacetylene welders toiled until dawn to effect repairs. It was worth sitting up all through a winter's night to enjoy this Son et Lumière spectacle, in spite of the cold in an unheated bedroom. I developed the technique of thawing a hole through the frosted windowpane so that I could the better observe proceedings. Unfortunately, Mother would rightly suspect what I was up to and would invariably burst unexpectedly into my bedroom saying, "You'll catch your death of cold", tucking me scoldingly back up in bed for my labours.

The following morning would offer the opportunity to make up with Mother for the previous night's delinquencies. One of our regular excursions would be to Henderson Row where the child welfare clinic was located opposite Edinburgh Academy. On the way we would pass the communal washhouse where women with squeaking pram chassis bearing tin tubs full of dirty laundry would congregate, each of them wearing a headscarf tied like a turban. A fag hanging from the lower lip tastefully complemented such fashionable millinery. Mother barely concealed her disdain for such people, referring to them as the *hoi polloi*, a term that I did not understand at the time. Mother also regarded the child clinic nearby with suspicion. Regular visits were occasioned by the need to collect supplies of cod liver oil and orange juice, as well as to present offspring for inspection by an expert on child development who would weigh the infants and enquire of mothers if they were experiencing any problems.

On one of our visits, I was later informed, Mother earnestly disclosed to the authorities there that I would happily drink milk from a bottle but not from a cup, whereas I would drink juice from a cup but not from a bottle. Matron, a stern and almost stereotypical authority figure, would have none of this nonsense, seizing upon Mother's preposterous suggestion which violated her received wisdom on child development. "An infant of that age can't tell the difference between milk and juice.", she scoffed. "Just leave him with me, and I'll soon enough have him drinking milk from a cup."

Mother retired to the garden at the back and spent a good half hour listening to my screams as Matron attempted to force milk down my throat from a cup. The milk went everywhere except where Matron wanted it to go. After half an hour or so, my face contorted with rage and soaked in tears, Matron conceded the point and summoned Mother to deliver her verdict: "Some infants are Conservative; others are Liberal, but this one's a die-hard." How prescient of her, but modern child psychology would acknowledge that the infant had deduced a rule: milk is drunk from a bottle; juice is drunk from a cup. I was simply demonstrating that I was following my own rule and equally objecting to anyone else having the temerity to violate it.

As an infant I was largely unaware of the effect of the war on those around me. Occasionally, however, the realities of warfare would intrude into the relative calm of home life. One of my most vivid memories is of being given a bath in front of the range in the living room. This was a weekly event, and it involved the laying out on the floor of a huge tarpaulin which my father had brought back from the Army one leave time. Upon this tarpaulin would be placed a pink papier maché bathtub which Mother would fill with warm water. I delighted in splashing the water everywhere, and always looked forward to bath-times.

One evening, as Mother was drying me down whilst I stood in the tub, she began to cry. I was unable to comfort her as I couldn't yet speak very well, but I wanted to say that everything was going to be all right. What I did not realise, but what I was told many years later, was that a news report on the radio had announced that my Father's regiment, along with others, was crossing the Rhine and that heavy casualties were expected. The next few days saw Mother subdued and preoccupied, but eventually a news bulletin reported a successful invasion with fewer casualties than had been anticipated, and Father eventually came home from leave bearing a torch and a model yacht for me to play with; then off again for what would mercifully seem like ages.

When Father was demobbed in 1946 he arrived home unexpectedly one day as he had done many times when previously on leave. However, for some reason this time he showed no signs of leaving after the customary day or two, and I became increasingly concerned that my perfect relationship with Mother was being sabotaged. I distinctly recall, when Mother and Father were locked in an embrace, pushing my way between their legs demanding to be included. One day, having had enough of this treatment, I asked Mother: "When's that man going to go away?" Her reply was chilling: "He lives here now, he's your Father." At that moment I felt that my innocence had ended and that in a real way my childhood had somehow come to a close after three only too brief years.

That this was not just paranoia on my behalf was reinforced quite unexpectedly one day when we had gone up to Princes Street to do some shopping. Now, a three year-old child's legs are not really capable of sustaining a walk of almost a mile without the need to pause to regain strength. My usual approach to this problem was simply to stop walking and to sit down on the pavement, whereupon Mother would immediately pick me up and carry me until I had recovered sufficiently to resume walking. That day my legs gave out and I sat down in anticipation of being gently lifted up and carried for a few minutes. Instead, I felt myself hoisted off my feet by Father's left hand whilst being delivered a whack across the bottom with the right. Such an approach may have encouraged me to walk for longer distances, but it clearly upset Mother as much as myself, and I recall the mixed feelings of anger, humiliation and resentment generated by such treatment.

Not long after, a similar incident occurred on an autumn day in the Botanic Gardens. Autumn was one of my favourite months, as the trees would shed their leaves, offering me the opportunity to kick around in them. On this particular day I decided that the landscape looked somewhat untidy, so I proceeded to fill one of the litterbins with fallen leaves. When the bin was full I stood back to admire my efforts, only to find myself being hoisted aloft and unceremoniously dumped in the litterbin on top of the leaves with my legs sticking out. I was well and truly wedged and when I looked up, there was Mr Burrows, Head Park-keeper, telling me that I deserved this new humiliation. I was furious and Mother told me later that she had never seen my face so red with rage. Laughin' on the ither side o' ma face I was, and by no means for the last time.

CHAPTER 2

THE IMMEDIATE POST-WAR YEARS

As I approached four years of age, Mother would send me downstairs to the Co-op store next door to buy potatoes and the occasional vegetable. I now recall the mystery of a 'forpit' of potatoes, which cost around sixpence. I can only guess that a forpit must have been shorthand for a fourth part, presumably of a stone, ie. three and a half pounds, which would last us all week. The Co-op had an impressive system of recording each and every transaction, no matter how insignificant it might have been. Money, together with a receipt, would be pushed into a metal tube and transported by an overhead wire to an office for processing. A few moments later, if you were lucky and the shop wasn't busy, back would come your change and a stamped receipt. This procedure always ensured that there was a decent-sized queue waiting, lending weight to the impression that the produce on sale was highly desirable and well worth waiting for, whereas in fact it was miserable and almost inedible, as practically all food was in wartime.

As I became adept at shopping locally on my own, I was allowed to extend my territory to across the road where Nairn's the Baker was located (now the Loon Fung Chinese restaurant) to buy a pan loaf. Crossing Howard Street in wartime was in no way hazardous as there were so few cars running and the tram made its imminent arrival known by several hundred clanking yards. The counter staff at Nairn's were invariably entertained by Mother's antics, as she was fanatical about keeping the windows clean, a task she undertook herself, both inside and out. The latter was made possible by the fact that the lower sash could be swung into the room once the counterweight had been removed and the frame secured in its anchorings. This enabled one to climb outside onto the window ledge. Mother would regularly step out onto the ledge of our second storey flat and proceed to wash the upper pane vigorously with no regard for her own safety. Nairn's staff would stand with their hearts in their mouths, distracted from serving waiting customers, as Mother worked her way round the three upper panes of the bay window.

I remember feeling immensely proud that Mother could achieve this feat on a regular basis without incident. Of course today, such behaviour would not be tolerated. First of all, the Police would have to be called to close the road to all passing traffic. Next, the Fire Brigade would have to be summoned to put up a ladder in anticipation of a rescue operation. And no doubt trained Counsellors would need to be brought in to talk Mother down from her perch or persuade her to go back inside the house. A Police caution would then inevitably follow if not an actual charge of a Public Order offence. But for Mother then it was simply all in a week's work.

As my independence increased, I began to be allowed to go out to play in Warriston Crescent across the road, in those days practically devoid of any cars parked in the street and with a stone horse trough at the end of the cul-de-sac which the Store milk horse used. I made friends with other children who played there, most of whom lived in the Crescent, although other children from nearby Howard Place were tolerated by the local residents. Initially, I played within sight of our house window, so that Mother could keep an eye on me from the front room. My first real friend was Marjerie Muir, whose parents ran a laundry business in a basement a few doors down from the Northern Bar (now rejoicing in the title 'The Orchard'). Marjerie was a bit of a tomboy, and we became good friends.

Play often consisted of idly watching the brewer's draymen lower barrels of beer down the chute into the pub cellar and actively playing games. Delivery of beer barrels was done manually, using ropes that the men let run through their huge leather aprons with which they protected their hands. We children would sit around waiting for the dray horse to pee, a spectacular sight, and our sex education pretty well began and perhaps even ended there. Peevers (hopscotch) was a popular game with the girls, but any boy caught playing it was regarded as a cissy. Tig was a gender free game whereas 'bools', or marbles, was played almost exclusively by boys. Skipping was a game strictly reserved for girls such as the Johnson sisters who lived next door to Marjerie. Skipping was invariably accompanied by a song to help along the rhythmic swing of the rope cranked by two girls whilst the skipper deftly avoided snagging her legs on the revolving rope.

Gradually, other children began to make themselves known to me and I was happy to play with anyone who happened to be out at the same time as I was. Another of my early years' friends was Michaelina, a Polish immigrant who lived with her parents in a basement flat opposite Marjerie's parents' laundry. Inhabiting a basement was regarded by Mother as a bit *infra dig* and not altogether in keeping with the respectable air that Warriston Crescent emanated on account of its association with such historical figures as Chopin. Michaelina had a better command of English than I had, being at the age of five a whole year older than I was. Mother always quizzed me about what Michaelina and I had been doing or talking about, and one day I informed her that Michaelina had called me a "Dirty wee bugger." Mother looked aghast and made no bones about the fact that that was what was called swearing, and could I ask Michaelina not to use such language. A few days later, Mother enquired as to what further exposure I might have had to such profanities, to be reassured: "She only said 'bugger' once!"

Class was not a concept entertained by a young child, and I became friends with children who lived in respectable Inverleith Row as well as at the 'scruffy' end of Warriston Crescent around the pub, the laundry and the piece of ground where the scaffies' barrows were kept. Scaffies (scavengers) were regarded by my parents as the lowest social class, and when I later attended school Father would warn me that if I did not stick at my lessons, I would inevitably face a life sentence of employment as a scaffie. We children used to play with the scaffies' barrows, wheeling them about like chariots, complete with their reeking contents of horse manure freshly swept from the street after the Co-op milk horse or brewer's dray had departed following their morning deliveries to homes and to the Northern Bar. Scaffies' barrows were great social levellers, although their use in this regard did not quite extend to the children who lived at the posher end of Warriston Crescent, children of whom we were somewhat wary on account of their more sophisticated speech and manners.

Playing around the mouth of Warriston Crescent led to the development of other casual friendships such as that of Stuart Harrod, whose father was the Landlord of the Northern Bar and who lived in the tied flat above the pub. Mr Harrod would pay Stuart and myself sixpence for cleaning up the mess on Saturday morning following the revelries of the night before when staff and punters alike would be rendered 'stocious' and incapable of anything but deep sleep. I will never forget the acrid smell of the cleaning fluid used to disinfect the place and sterilise the beer pipes. The money earned at the pub exceeded my thruppence pocket money and enabled me to purchase a large flat bread from Nairn's which I would put 'up my juke', soon to be enjoyed perched at the top of one of the trees in Warriston Crescent. Given the grinding poverty that I had been born into, I learned early in life that any small rewards for honest toil should be celebrated; a philosophy that I have retained throughout adulthood.

Another casual friend for a few years was Jackie Summers, who lived in Howard Place close to a house formerly inhabited a century before by Robert Louis Stevenson. Tree climbing on the piece of wasteland next to the bowling club was an activity at which a number of us came to excel, and Jackie Summers, Stuart Harrod and myself jointly held the climbing record, both in terms of height and speed. We soon came to be recognised as the 'experts' and as such recognised that girls were pretty useless at tree climbing, so we would coax them into acts of bravery in which they would not themselves have otherwise engaged without the social stigma of failure in the eyes of the self-appointed 'experts'. Of course the inevitable happened: one day Marjerie got stuck three quarters of the way up and froze with fear. The Fire Brigade was duly summoned whereupon the 'experts' ran away and hid lest Marjerie should successfully pin the blame on us for her predicament.

As I grew older I began to tire of the company of many of the local children. Marjerie, however, in spite of being the daughter of a laundress, always appeared intelligent and creative, and we continued our friendship for many years until my parents moved to Warriston. As a rare treat in the school summer holidays, Marjerie's father would take me in his Morris Eight van to help him deliver laundry, and when I returned home I felt that I had been accepted into the Muir family and Marjerie came to feel more like a sister than just a friend. We used to exchange jokes and make up stories together. When we were older, about seven or eight years, Marjerie's finest hour was when she made up a scurrilous poem about Jackie Summers. It went: "Jackie-wackie did a kackie on his mother's knee; His mother said: "You naughty boy, you'll eat it for your tea!" I fell in love with Marjerie at that moment, but I don't expect she ever knew because either I never told her or I never knew myself what love was.

With growing confidence I ventured further down Warriston Crescent and encountered children who had possessions that I could only dream of, such as a 'guider', a tricycle or bicycle. Guiders were homemade wooden carts mounted on pram wheels, which could be steered by swivelling the front axle. Owning one meant that one was at least lower middle class, as working class pram frames were invariably converted into vehicles to take the tin tub of dirty clothes to the 'Steamie' (wash-house) in Henderson Row. I was always trying to scrounge a ride on someone's guider or trike, but since I could not reciprocate with anything other than my native wit, which was invariably unappreciated, the other children soon tired of me.

As the years went by I gradually became aware that I was different, both from the 'scruffy' types I felt I had little in common with on account of their roughness, but also from the 'posh' types whose material wealth overwhelmed me. I encountered two Warriston Crescent families who fell into the 'posh' category: the Kuenssbergs and the Kemps. Dr Kuenssberg was a Physician, and Mr Kemp was reputed amongst us to do nothing as he didn't go to work as other fathers did. I believe that the BBC Political Journalist Laura Kuenssberg may be the grand-daughter of Dr Kuenssberg and the daughter of his son Nikki Kuenssberg who was a few years older than I was and who played with Robbie and Arnold Kemp, neighbours a few doors along the Crescent.

As I recall, there were four Kemp children: Robbie, David, Arnold and Christina. Arnold later went on to do great things in journalism, working for 'The Guardian', editing 'The Scotsman' and taking a keen interest in Scottish affairs until his untimely death at the age of sixty-three. He mentioned our tenement block in his book 'The Hollow Drum', referring to its inhabitants as 'working class, Conservative voting, God-fearing and law-abiding'. Had he known us better he would have realised that Mr Murdoch, a pharmacist, and my Father, a legal clerk lived in such houses, and that I myself 'enjoyed', if that's not too much of an exaggeration, a private education at George Heriot's School. He would also have been lost for words had I been able to inform him that my Mother was currently producing one of his father's plays at Broughton Place Church, but the opportunity somehow never presented itself.

Had they lived to read Arnold's book my parents would have been shocked to see him describe them as 'working class'. Indeed they distanced themselves socially from 'common types', as they would call them, such as those who frequented the Northern Bar on their way to 'the dogs' (greyhound racing) at Powderhall Stadium. My Father once pointed out those cloth-capped figures to me from our sitting room window as they came out of the pub. "See these people," he would say, "They're going to the dogs!" Father meant this metaphorically as well as literally, but the meaning and the moral were both lost on me until many years later when that expression became familiar.

Unusually, the Kemp sister Christina once deigned to speak to me one day, and as she seemed approachable rather than snooty, I was happy to strike up a conversation with her. She probably thought that someone wearing a Heriot's uniform couldn't really be a toerag and was no doubt vetting me as a potential friend. At any rate, she casually asked what my Father did for a living. I told her that he worked at the National Guarantee and Suretyship Association whose offices were in Charlotte Square, which I felt would suitably impress her. In return, I asked what her father did, as he seemed to spend all his time at home doing nothing. Christina told me that he was a playwright, whereupon I made the fatal error of 'correcting' her by saying that she meant to say a 'play writer'. The look of utter contempt that she silently flung me yet burns deeply in my psyche, and regrettably we never spoke again. Aye, laughin' on the ither side o' ma face I was.

The Kemp and Kuenssberg children played in the school playing fields opposite their homes and it became clear to me that they inhabited a rich world of play to which I had no access on account of having little or no pocket money to spend. For example I used to watch in fascination as Meccano rocket launchers would be constructed bearing beautifully built paper rockets powered by Jetex engines. Such do-it-yourself playthings would be forever out of reach of mere guttersnipes such as myself, and I soon formed an image of my proper place in society. That I was never invited to share in such play reinforced my view, and gradually I began to grasp the painful fact that although I was not as low in social status as the *hoi polloi* that Mother referred to, I was unmistakably lower than those who inhabited the Georgian crescent in which I played.

Warriston Crescent held occasional surprises. One day, the Water of Leith inundated the back gardens of the entire crescent and we watched with awe as furniture floated about in basements full of brown water. I have since ascertained that this event took place in 1947 when I was four. The fire brigade did its best to clean up the mess but not before considerable damage had been done to the properties. Rumour was that a resident who kept ducks had removed some stones from their back garden wall to allow the birds to drink from the river. When it ran in spate after a prolonged period of rain, it burst through the gap, flooding garden after garden until the basements of all of the houses flooded, furniture bobbing about on the surface of brown water. I often wonder whose insurers paid out for the damage, but at the time the rumour developed that Arnold Kemp had had a hand in the disaster, having assisted in making the hole in the first place!

As I grew older I used to look forward to making a visit to Nana's shop on my own, as it was filled with playthings. Although the shop was very small by any standards, it contained shelves full of sweets of all descriptions, and cigarettes with exotic names such as Craven A (Will Not Affect The Throat), Gold Flake, Paffing Cloud (the obsolete 'f' was used as an 's') and Three Castles. A rare treat for me was when a 'traveller" (sales representative) would call, leaving behind 'dummies' (fake chocolates) for display in the window. These were fashioned out of wood set in traditional wrappers, and there would always be plenty of them left over, enabling me to open my own 'sweetie shop' which I laid out on a tray in the back shop with Nana playing customer. Serried ranks of Fry's Five Boys, Mars Bars and chocolate peppermint creams would be set out, and 'retailing' these would keep me occupied for a whole morning as it involved such mental arithmetic and applied mathematics as calculating how much change to give out of a ten bob note (the equivalent of 50p today) for three items costing sixpence-ha'penny each.

Nana also made her own sweets to supplement her modest income. Tablet (the Scottish equivalent of fudge) was a regular standby, but Nana also made 'toffee doddles'. These were made out of boiled brown sugar and water with a dash of vinegar added. The solution would be heated up in a large black pan on the range in the back shop and boiled until it reached a toffee consistency. Nana would then pour out the contents of the pan onto a marble-topped table and proceed, with her bare hands, to form the pool of boiling hot toffee into a long sausage. After a few minutes the toffee would begin to solidify, whereupon Nana would take a pair of kitchen scissors and cut the roll into pyramids. When cooled, these were then bagged up and sold for thruppence a quarter. Toffee doddles were one of my favourite sweets, even though I knew that the sack of brown sugar under the counter was home to families of mice whose black droppings had to be carefully sifted from the sugar before each boiling. There was no Health and Safety in those days of war and we civilians lived comparatively dangerously as the Nanny State had yet to be invented.

When Nana eventually retired from the sweetie shop in her late sixties, she had no savings to speak of and no pension other than that from the State. Mother managed to find her a room in a flat in Eildon Street where she lived for a few years. I am unaware of who paid the rent as her pension wouldn't have covered it, but Mother probably did to Father's annoyance. Nana then moved to another flat in Arboretum House at the entrance to the Botanics where I used to visit her regularly. One evening there came a telephone call from Edinburgh Royal Infirmary, summoning my parents there as Nana had been rushed into A & E and had then been admitted to one of the wards. I was worried, and sat disconsolately beside the fire looking at the clock every few minutes. At eight-twenty I checked the time on and put some more coal on the fire because the room was beginning to feel distinctly chilly.

A few minutes later I glanced at the clock again: still eight-twenty! I was feeling cold and the fire looked as if it was dying so I stirred it up with the poker and put more coal on it. The room began to take on an eerie stillness and distinct coldness and silence. Eventually my parents came home at around ten o'clock looking shattered. My Mother's first words were: "It's all over now". I said, "Yes, I know, Nana died at twenty past eight." Mother looked shocked, and recomposing herself said, "Yes, her last words were, 'I feel a cold wind passing over me'", and that her death had been recorded as eight-twenty, the very same time at which the clock had apparently stopped, the room chilled and the fire almost extinguished in spite of my best efforts to keep it going.

Two further incidents were to mark the end of a second golden age of childhood innocence for me. One evening Mother told me that someone from the Church called Miss Mackie would be calling to speak to me. This intelligence was met with a strong feeling of foreboding, and not without good cause as it turned out. Miss Mackie duly arrived the following evening and began to tell me all about the Sunday school she ran. As I was now four years old, I was eligible to attend. As I recall, I displayed complete indifference to this generous offer, but before I could open my mouth Mother spoke up on my behalf, saying that she would be honoured to have me attend. I personally felt that I had been fitted up, but refusal was not an option at the age of four and in the years of post-war austerity children were supposed to be grateful for any mercies offered them.

The following Sunday I was dragged off to church at Broughton Place, an imposing neo-classical edifice (now an international auction house, God replaced by Mammon) where the Reverend George S Gunn, Doctor of Divinity, preached his carefully prepared forty-five minute sermons from which I was initially spared until I left Sunday School. Between eleven and eleven thirty I would be forced to sit in a cold pew beside my parents listening to Dr Gunn droning on in his elocutioned, 'Cheuchter' voice, as Father described it (a Cheuchter refers to someone with a Highland as opposed to a Lowland accent). I had the misfortune to be seated at a pew adjacent to an elderly woman whom I had overheard Mother say suffered from 'a woman's problem'. I diagnosed that one in two seconds, given my early familiarity with the smell of ammonia and the knowledge of its source and, after making my protests public, Mother kindly agreed to swap places with me to spare my sensibilities. Sundays were thereafter a source of dread to me, not to mention the fact that I had to walk all the way to and from church in every weather, invariably returning to a late lunch of cold mutton with white fat on it which Father assured me was 'good for you'.

Miss Mackie's Sunday School was occasionally a source of misinformation to my tender ears. One Sunday morning, just before Christmas, we were told that Jesus had been born in the stable. I did not hear this quite correctly, and immediately rushed home to announce proudly that Jesus had been born 'on this table'. My pride at believing that the Deity Himself in His infinite wisdom should have chosen our humble Sunday School for His son's nativity was gently eroded by my disbelieving parents, who probably thought that I was simply trying to wind them up, whereas I merely wished to share my joy at this revelation.

The following week yet another misunderstanding was communicated to me at Sunday School. One of my favourite hymns was 'Away in a Manger', and I liked it so much that I memorised it. One of the lines ran: 'Bless all the dear children in Thy tender care, and fit us for Heaven to live with Thee there.' No-one ever bothered to explain who 'Thee There' was, but because both names contained the word 'the' I assumed that he must be some sort of bear like Winnie The Pooh, a preposterous notion from which my parents soon disabused me. So that from the tender age of four I began to distrust anything that adults told me; a sceptical attitude that was to serve me well in adulthood.

When Mother saw that I loved singing she was pleased because she was herself an accomplished pianist who could read sheet music effortlessly. Nana also played the piano, accompanying herself to folk songs such as 'Caller Herring'. Even although she could not read music she could play a tune with both hands after hearing it just the once. Father, on the other hand, had van Gogh's ear for music, and in church he would content himself with miming, occasionally feeling confident enough or forgetting himself sufficiently to produce a bum note, whereupon he would invariably fall silently back into mime. Father's total lack of musical ability did not, however, prevent him from acting as the severest self-appointed critic of the church organist, poor mildly-mannered Mr Cresswell, whose approach to choir training had apparently led Father into such a bitter disagreement with the Authorities over his appointment that he had felt honour bound to relinquish his church eldership.

From then on, Father considered that it was his unelected and unpaid role to scrutinise Mr Cresswell's playing from our pew at the front row of the upstairs gallery, making his disapproval of Mr Cresswell's performance evident to all. He would often complain that the poor man was drowning out the congregation by a too enthusiastic application of the swell pedal. He also held the opinion that the Faux Bourdon stop should only be used for special effects rather on a regular basis, failing to understand that this was Mr Cresswell's signature style of playing. As even the most restrained form of musical accompaniment, I felt, would have adumbrated Father's mime performances, I didn't really see what he had to complain about.

Mother was always embarrassed by Father's impromptu duties as resident music critic, and she tried to distance herself from his disapproving gaze and *sotto voce* asides. Being wedged shoulder to shoulder in a pew next to him made this difficult for her, but she nonetheless managed to carry it off, conveying her sentiments by subtle use of what little body language was available to her, such as an almost imperceptible turn of the head away from Father, accompanied by glances heavenward. Mercifully I would be spared further embarrassment when I filed out of the church along with the other four year olds to join Miss Mackie's Sunday School class at eleven thirty before Dr Gunn commenced delivery of his forty-five minute sermon, deeply steeped in well-researched Theology.

As we lived just along the road from the Royal Botanic Garden, it was always available to us within five minutes' walk from our house. Once demobbed, Father taught me how to feed the birds by hand by keeping ever so still, and I was thus able to coax great tits, blue tits, coal tits, chaffinches and robins onto the palm of my outstretched hand with breadcrumbs and pieces of cheese. This engendered in me an early love of wild life and for a city child it was a good learning experience. During and after the War many men well past conscription age could be seen feeding the birds, but this is no longer a fashionable occupation, although one can now see children feeding nuts to the squirrels.

In those early post-war days there was little by way of entertainment available, and what there was, was by and large unaffordable to us; so people had to make their own. The Church offered the opportunity of putting on amateur dramatic productions in its hall next door, and such activities brightened up the cold winter evenings before the days of television. Mother became a leading light at such events, not only taking, or rather giving herself the lead female part in many one-act plays, by rising as far as the rank of Producer of a play which was performed at one of the Edinburgh amateur drama festivals. When the Edinburgh Evening News drama critic Michael Howard subsequently panned it, Mother wrote a sharp riposte which the paper dutifully published the following day. Lest anyone doubt the story, I still possess the cuttings!

Broughton Place Church hosted a wide variety of social events. My Auntie Jean was Secretary of the Women's Temperance Association and Mother was a leading light in the Amateur Dramatic Society. The Church had Cubs, Scouts, Brownies and Girl Guides, and all sorts of social activities took place under its auspices, such as jumble sales to raise money for foreign missions. The photo overleaf shows a number of Church Officers outside the Church. In the centre, kneeling, is the Reverend Dr George S Gunn and to the right of him in the picture is my Uncle Willie, Assistant Church Organist. Fourth from the left in the second row, Auntie Jean can be seen smiling: a fast shutter speed must have been needed to capture that expression as her habitual one was of stern disapproval.

I am not one hundred per cent sure if the Church missionary, Miss Dorothy Wallace, appears in the picture, but the lady in the checked jacket second from the left in the second row rings a bell with me. In any event, even if it isn't her, it is worth mentioning that the Church was very proud of the support it gave to missionary work abroad. Every few months Dr Gunn would read out from the pulpit a letter that Miss Wallace had sent home, bringing us news from the Darjeeling Eastern Himalayan Diocese where she was based. Father always maintained that Miss Wallace had 'a touch of the tar brush' about her on account of her swarthy complexion, but that didn't stop him from dipping into his pocket when a special collection was taken up for her work.

Uncle Willie would also participate in the dramatic activities that regularly took place. I never ceased to be amazed at how such familiar family members could be so transformed in their identities once they took to the stage, complete with props, make-up and lighting effects, that they became believable alter egos. Those dramatic activities provided me with the dubious treat of having to listen to Mother learn her lines, with me holding the script while she perfected some nuance of delivery. By the time the play was performed I knew her part as word perfect as she did, together with all the other lines, which made the opening night somewhat of an anticlimax. But I enjoyed the dress rehearsals where I would assist Father behind the scenes in his role as Lighting Engineer: one that he took very seriously. Father had an unorthodox approach to diagnosing whether current was flowing through a wire or not: if, on touching it on an earthed surface a shower of sparks flew, then current was deemed to be flowing!

Uncle Willie worked at the Head Office of the Ben Line Shipping Company. His job was to select crew members and this led to his being cultivated by a certain Captain Liston, who would regularly invite us all down for Sunday lunch to Leith Docks whenever a Ben Line ship was in port. I will never forget the delicious smell and taste of the freshly baked dinner rolls that were made by the Chinese cooks in the galley, and the chicken soup was also out of this world to my palate. By buttering up my Uncle in this way, Captain Liston successfully prevailed upon him to select the crew that he himself wanted, rather than having Head Office's wishes foisted off on him.

In those days anyone without a car, and that must have amounted to most people, had to use either the tram or the bus for transport. Trams were for relatively short journeys; buses for longer ones. In the late 1940s we were still able to get a tram from Canonmills to the terminus at Liberton Dams, about half a mile from where my grandparents lived. But then we would have to walk that half mile from the terminus to their house so that the whole journey took the best part of an hour. Saturday afternoons were reserved for such visits and in anticipation of our visit my Grandfather would spend the whole morning in the kitchen baking gingerbread, sponges, scones and pancakes. As Granny was a chronic asthmatic she was treated practically as an invalid, so that Grandpa had done the cooking all his married life: not bad for a pre-feminist Victorian.

Grandpa owned a dog named Dandy, an Airedale terrier with a formidable intelligence and a sweet nature. Dandy would permit me to sit on his back and transport me around the room and I never heard him as much as growl. Dandy's skills were legendary. He could carry an egg in his mouth without breaking it, but equally he could grind a bone to powder if he put his mind to it. He was alleged to be a good rabbiter and Grandpa would take him walking on the Pentlands every weekend. He told me that when he and Dandy were younger he would walk so far that he had to carry an exhausted Dandy back home. When Dandy died Grandpa exhibited more grief than when his own wife died, and that's the sad truth of the matter.

As Grandpa grew older he recruited Dandy to assist with his shopping. Dandy would be given a bag to carry in his mouth, containing a purse and a shopping list. He would then be pointed down the road to the top of Liberton Brae where he would scratch at the door of the first shop. The shopkeeper would open the door, let Dandy in, and open the bag to read the note and see what was wanted. With the goods placed in the bag and the right money taken, Dandy would be shown into the shop next door, and so on until all the shops had been visited. Then Dandy would carry the shopping back to Grandpa who would check the purse for change to see that he hadn't been swindled by any of the shopkeepers.

So reliable was Dandy at these errands that when the farmer at the top of the road telephoned to offer him a free chicken, Grandpa duly sent Dandy up the road with a bag in his mouth. To his dying day Grandpa never did understand what happened to that chicken as he never received it, but twenty years later I accidentally found out from his nextdoor neighbour who had been an eye-witness to the event and who had kept it to himself all these years. Apparently Dandy had been spotted trotting along the pavement towards Grandpa's house, bag in mouth. As he approached, he got down on his belly and wriggled past the gate, having worked out that he could not be seen so easily. Once past the gate Dandy opened the bag and scoffed the whole chicken!

Other, more human deceptions were perpetrated, even by myself. One day Mother told me that she and Father were going to the 'pictures', meaning the local cinema, and that Auntie Jean had been prevailed upon to babysit. This came as chilling news to me, and I pondered as to how I might manage to impress her; perhaps even convince her to some small extent that I was not as evil as I felt she believed I was, and certainly not at all deserving of some anticipated and inevitable punishment. When bedtime came, Auntie Jean asked what I usually did: have a drink, have a read? I immediately responded that I always read the Bible before going to sleep. Mightily impressed, Auntie Jean fetched our family bible, asking me if I had a favourite chapter. "Ruth!" I immediately piped up, believing that not only would she take this as evidence of a precocious erudition that deserved respect, but that she would also be flattered by the fact that, as everyone knows, the Old Testament book had been named after her own daughter, my Cousin Ruth. I soon nodded off to her dronings and awakened the next morning, surprised to find that I still retained two arms, two legs and a head. Auntie Jean had fallen for it, and I had survived! What I hadn't counted on, of course, was that my parents would later interrogate Auntie Jean on their return, asking had I been well behaved or not. They met Auntie Jean's account of my religious fervour with incredulity and shame at my untruthfulness, and the next day when they confronted me with my deception I soon enough found myself laughin' on the ither side o' ma face.

As Grandpa reached his mid-eighties and his spinster daughter, my Auntie Bessie who lived with him, retired from the Civil Service, time to themselves became available, and no doubt an element of boredom eventually set in. So Grandpa decided that he would like to see a bit of the world, and he persuaded Auntie Bessie to book them both on a three-week Mediterranean cruise on the SS Orsova. This was to prove an excellent decision and, when they returned, although Grandpa had possessed no hair beyond the age of twenty-five, he now sported a head of fine white down. The following year they both took another cruise, this time on the SS Orcades, and Auntie Bessie sent me a postcard from every port at which they disembarked.

To Grandpa's disappointment, no further hair growth took place the second time round and that was his last cruise. I last saw Grandpa on one summer's evening when I had cycled all the way from Inverleith to Liberton. He was surprised but pleased to see me as this was an unusual trip, undertaken in the middle of the week on my own initiative rather than my parents' ritualised Saturday visit. Why I felt the need to visit him remains a mystery to me, but I'm glad I did. When I arrived he wasn't his usual self and he told me that he had had 'a funny turn' the night before. I said I was sorry to hear it and when I left I assured him that I was looking forward to seeing him again soon. His resigned reply, "I hope so.", worried me and I told my parents that they should visit him because I feared the worst. They didn't, and Grandpa died two days later, mercifully in his sleep. He was just short of ninety years old: a great age for anyone in 1957 and far in excess of a life expectancy of sixty-eight years, which was par for the course in those days.

CHAPTER 3

THE SCHOOL YEARS

When I reached the age of four Mother began to talk to me about going to day school. Heriot's was mentioned as Uncle Willie had been a pupil there and priority was allegedly given to children whose relatives had attended the school. Applications had to be made a year before the starting date, and one day Mother announced that I was to go up to Heriot's for an interview. I was carefully briefed about being polite and after lunch we boarded a tram for the journey up to Lauriston Place. On our way across the playground Mother pointed out the cycle sheds that were enclosed by wire mesh. My opinion was that they were where the monkeys were kept, despite Mother's attempt to disabuse me of this fantastic notion. I was soon introduced to a nice lady called Miss Redman who was the Head of the Preparatory Department. Miss Redman, as her name suggested to me, bore a very flushed complexion. She proceeded to put me at my ease and then said that she was going to ask me to do a few things for her. Mother was ushered from the room and the entrance examination duly commenced.

My first task was to take a piece of string and to thread a series of round and square coloured wooden beads onto it to make a pattern that Miss Redman showed me using her beads. This appeared to me to be so childishly simple that I completed it in seconds. She then asked me to hold up my string of beads so that she could check out my handiwork. As I did so, disaster struck: all the beads fell off and rolled about the floor. Seeing that I was laughin' on the ither side o' ma face, Miss Redman apologised profusely to me for not having knotted the string, but deep down I felt that I had failed to spot the deliberate mistake, which was the true purpose of the exercise. It was only decades later as a Psychology postgraduate that I would come across the test materials that Miss Redman had administered to me as a child: the Weschler Infant and Pre-School Intelligence Test. And it is the Examiner's job to tie a knot in the string for the child, so there!

Despondent, I was reunited with Mother and we both went into the Headmaster's study for a personal interview. The School might have thought itself up to date with psychometric selection procedures, but the Headmaster was more of a traditionalist himself, and he insisted on conducting his own personal assessments of potential pupils. William McLaren Dewar wore his graduation robes and mortarboard as outward symbols of both his intellectual superiority and high social status. He was seated at his desk by the window of a room that overlooked Edinburgh Castle, and Mother glanced at me apprehensively as the gowned and mortared presence commenced his interrogation. "How did you come to the School?", he asked, "By bus or by tram?" "By tram" I replied. "Did you go inside or upstairs?" "Inside.", I replied. "What was the number of the tram?", he enquired. "I don't know, how could I see the number when I was inside!" Mother looked as if she wished a hole in the floor to open up, and for either herself, me or both of us to be swallowed up by it.

"Well then," said Mr Dewar, briskly changing tack, "Do you see that castle out of the window there?" "Yes.", I replied. "Well, did you know that it is my castle?", he asked. "That's not your castle!", I exclaimed in astonishment at such a ridiculous suggestion. "Then whose castle is it?", he enquired. "The King's castle!", I confidently retorted, giving him a withering look as if he was some sort of cretin. Mother was by now completely distraught and I instinctively knew that I had failed another important test of character and no doubt yet again brought shame upon the family. I felt that the hand of history had decreed that my role in life was to be a trouble-maker, a feeling that Mother did nothing to dispel when she related the whole episode to Father after tea.

On returning home from work, Father seemed unusually curious as to how things had gone at the school and when Mother gave him no hope of my ever being accepted on account of my disastrous performance earlier, to my surprise, instead of scolding me, he actually looked quite pleased. I was later to learn that he had never wanted me to have a private education but had hoped that I would attend the local Broughton School as he himself had done. However, in spite of all portents to the contrary, to everyone's surprise, a few days later an offer of a place at Heriot's arrived through the post, and in 1948 I commenced formal education, initially under the care of Miss Murray who ran Class A. I remember overhearing Mother having a talk with Father about having to cut down on their smoking in order to pay the school fees. It seemed to me that Father was always very grumpy after that and in fact did not quit smoking until after I had left school. He evidently placed the value of the certainty of his addiction at least as high as the uncertainty of the outcome my education, and as events were to turn out, who could have blamed him?

The photo below shows me at around the age of six or seven wearing my school tie and pullover. The picture was taken on the day of my Grandparents' Golden Wedding. I am seated on Auntie Jean's knee next to Grandpa and Granny. In the back row from left to right are Cousin Ruth, Father, Auntie Bessie, Uncle Willie and Mother. The picture was taken by my Father using a tripod, and the delayed action setting on his camera gave him time to dash round into the picture himself. Father also printed the photo which remains remarkably bright and unfaded after sixty years, a tribute to his photographic skills.

At Heriot's, Miss Murray was a wonderfully kind and natural teacher. She possessed a strap, as did all the teachers, but she hardly ever used it. On the one occasion that she did, its use was probably justified by the pupils' bad behaviour. A classmate by the name of Lindsay Watt, a large child by anybody's standards, was victimised and bullied simply because of his relative size. We five year olds would chant at him: "Old Granny Witchie!" a term nobody would own up to inventing, mainly because of its utter naffness. But unknown to us, our taunts had been observed by Miss Murray from her classroom window as we played outside. On return to the classroom after the two minute interval, each of us was lined up to receive a very gentle stroke of the tawse which did not hurt in the least, and most of us were so ashamed at being strapped at all that the lesson had been already learned.

In Miss Murray's class we were taught to read by means of visual aids. One of the first sentences we had to learn to read was printed on a large poster-like sheet suspended over the blackboard easel. A garishly coloured lithograph of a bird bore beneath it the words in large letters: "The little robin sat on the branch and sang." I was amazed that the letters 'ch' had to be pronounced 'sh', and I couldn't wait to get home to catch Mother out by asking her how she would pronounce 'branch'. I was bitterly disappointed to find out that she already knew and I felt that no amount of education would ever make me as wise as her.

The highlight of the end of my first school year was to be given the leading part in a play entitled: "The Dragon who Liked Cake". As I had been presciently cast as the King, I clearly needed a crown.

The school seemed to think that it was my parents' job to provide this stage prop and Mother and Father both set about constructing one out of metal foil with coloured beads sewn onto it. Crown construction took several nights before both were satisfied but the result was most impressive. My parents subsequently complained bitterly when the item was not returned after what was to be the first and final performance of this thespian event. In retrospect, being robbed of the crown that patently belonged to me and my family was to become a metaphor for my future academic life, and it was not for many years that I was to reclaim it legitimately in adulthood.

At the end of my first year at school I was surprised but pleased to receive First Prize in the form of a book entitled "The Twins at Hillside Farm." I still have the book and I recall running home proudly holding it and then reading it right through in about half an hour. The following year I entered Class C, run by Mrs Anderson. Mrs Anderson, in my view, was a horrid, sadistic woman who took an immediate dislike to me. Winning first prize and being given the leading part in the school play the previous year in Mrs Anderson's eyes evidently demanded that she engineer a fall from grace, lest my childish hubris take root, and she was determined to knock the wind out of my sails, a task at which in the event she eminently succeeded.

In Mrs Anderson's class I became such a bag of nerves that I developed various facial tics for which she would reproach me in front of the class. She even went as far as writing a letter to my parents offering them her own tentative diagnosis of St Vitus' Dance. Today a teacher would be sacked for such unprofessional behaviour, and I often wonder if she had had the authority to act in this way. On receipt of the letter Mother duly panicked and instead of making an immediate complaint to the Headmaster as any parent of today would do, she prevailed upon Dr Thorpe to refer me to a Paediatrician at the Sick Children's Hospital, a Dr Eric Dott as he turned out to be; brother of Professor Norman Dott the eminent Neurosurgeon. Dr Dott examined me and simply said that the child was highly strung. Over the next few years I was to see Dr Dott again, but mercifully under more favourable and social, as opposed to professional circumstances.

During my period of study in Class C, I became friendly with Brian Smith, now the Bishop of Edinburgh. Brian's parents were very pushy and they used to telephone mine on a regular basis to try to find out if I was receiving special coaching as Brian had come second to me the year before, when they clearly thought that he should have come first. Father used to fob them off with some story or other, and he was clearly irritated by the intrusion, but it became clear to me that academic competitiveness had taken hold, at least in parental eyes. Later it was to be revealed that Mrs Anderson was a good friend of Brian Smith's parents and, no surprises here, at the end of the year Brian was awarded First Equal prize with myself on Mrs Anderson's personal recommendation. I had been fitted up again and the facial tics increased in frequency and intensity.

On leaving the Preparatory Department we were all streamed, presumably on the basis of our academic performance. There were three streams representing intellectual ability The clever Dicks were put into Class 1L; the mediocre Dicks into Class 2L and the thick

Dicks into Class 3L, or at least that's how it seemed to me at the time. Brian Smith and I of course went into 1L, along with a few others, where life was so uneventful that I recall precisely nothing of note that year other than a sense of welcome respite from Mrs Anderson's evil clutches, and the irritating tics rapidly disappeared without medical intervention. At the end of that academic year I received Second prize with The Bishop receiving First. Home swatting was evidently paying off in the Smith household, thanks to Father having said that I undertook one hour of homework every night, a target that Brian's parent's evidently believed and which they encouraged Brian to emulate.

After 1L, Brian and I went up to 4L, which was Miss Hamilton's class. Miss Hamilton had taught in Canada and had been trained in what I now recognise to be the Froebel method. Miss Hamilton's class was without doubt the most exciting in the whole of the Junior School. Not only did we each have the opportunity of weaving a scarf on her loom (which I still have, the scarf that is), we were taught grammar by means of a set of symbols, whereby a noun would be represented by a red triangle; a preposition by a yellow banana, a verb by an orange circle, and so on. Above each word in the sentence that Miss Hamilton would write on the blackboard she would draw above a symbol appropriate to its grammatical category. For practice, she would write up more sentences, asking us each in turn to draw the correct symbol above each word. I cannot recall anyone who failed to grasp the system, and Miss Hamilton's method was highly successful in turning a highly abstract concept such as a part of speech into a concrete referent, thereby helping the child to fix the concept in his mind.

Two decades later, when I was an undergraduate student of Psychology at Edinburgh University, our lecturer was clearly struggling to teach us Chomsky's system of transformational grammar, which was very new and radical, and we were equally struggling to get our heads around it. One night after grappling with this stuff unsuccessfully all day, I went to bed exhausted. In my sleep I had a dream in which I went into a market and purchased some apples, oranges and bananas, which I put into a brown paper bag. When I later put my hand into the bag to take out a fruit it had been transformed into a different fruit. I immediately awakened with a full grasp of transformational grammar and the following day I became sought after by other students as I was the only one who had managed to work it out. Thank you Miss Hamilton, if you only knew what genius you possessed!

The next move up the school was to Class 6L with Miss Dixon: Dixon the Vixen, as we knew her. Miss Dixon was short and stout and came across as severe and punitive. She was a committed convert to the power of the strap, to which she had frequent recourse. Miss Dixon had an interested strapping technique. As she brought the strap down forcibly on tender palms her right knee would flex upwards as if to add power to the blow, or perhaps more charitably, to maintain her equilibrium, such was the effort she put into the delivery. My classmate Frank Scott became adept at moving his hand sideways at the last moment, causing Miss Dixon to produce a self-inflicted knee injury, but nobody dared laugh, such was the fear she engendered as her wrath visibly increased. I don't think she had ever read that one should never strike a child in anger.

Miss Dixon ran a spelling bee in which each pupil had to come up with a tricky word which the rest of the class had to spell correctly. I found the whole thing a bit boring and beneath me, so I resolved to find a really difficult word for the following day. Working as he did in legal circles, Father was always a reliable source of arcane and difficult to spell words, and he suggested that I offer the word 'desiccated' to the class, which I duly did. After many unsuccessful attempts at getting the spelling right, and much muttering amongst disgruntled class members, Miss Dixon eventually intervened and asked me how I would spell it. When I did she said that I had got it wrong and that it should have two 's's and one 'c'.

Returning home that evening Father asked me if anyone had got 'desiccated' right, to which I replied that he must have got it wrong in the first place because Miss Dixon had said so. Father, infuriated by Miss Dixon's audacity to contradict his sound scholarship, immediately fetched the dictionary, pointing out the correct spelling and insisting that I take the dictionary into school with me to educate Miss Dixon. The following day I felt fortunate that I hadn't been tawsed for my insolence. I learned two lessons that day: never ask Father for difficult spelling words, and never trust teachers. Oh, and a third: no one likes a smart Alec.

One good thing about school was the summer holidays, which seemed to go on for many long, hot weeks, as memory serves to distort the fact that it was not always sunny in Edinburgh. As we grew older, at around the age of eight, my friend Marjerie and I would take our spades and pails on a tram down to Granton where we would alight and proceed to do some beach combing. I was always interested in nature and fancied myself as a bit of an expert on the subject. I was delighted one day to be given the opportunity of demonstrating my encyclopaedic knowledge of sea life to Marjerie by showing her the remains of 'sea-cucumbers' which littered the beach, and we raced to fill our pails with these fine specimens which we took home in the tram, much to the other passengers' amusement. On returning home, Mother, on the other hand, was not at all amused, and she immediately threw the whole lot out in the bin, much to my disappointment. Many years later I was again to encounter such 'species' by way of the Durex dispensing machine in the gents' toilet of the Northern Bar.

After Class 6L came 9L, run by Lieutenant Commander Ross-Gaul, the scourge of the Junior school and our first male teacher, whose name was enough to fill one with apprehension. Ross-Gaul's first task was to introduce us to his strap with great ceremony, pointing out that it had two tawse, but because he was such a kind and gentle child-loving teacher, he would only use half the strap on any one occasion. However, we were informed that we had to keep a note of the number of 'half skelps' we received in order at the end of the year to receive the balance that he had kindly spared us. I actually believed him, and recorded each and every half strapping assiduously in my homework notebook, looking forward to the last day of term with dread. The threat was apparently never carried out, as the administration of some eighty odd half skelps owed to me throughout the year would surely have been classed as actual bodily harm, but I skipped school that day just to be on the safe side.

Ross-Gaul spent as little time as he could in the classroom, preferring instead to busy himself with matters relating to the running of the Combined Cadet Force. His usual approach to teaching was to write on the board a number of pages from an Arithmetic book, leave the class for half an hour and return to skelp all those who had not completed a sufficient number of sums to his satisfaction. Fortunately, I never received a skelp for Arithmetic, which I loved, but others weren't so lucky. When there was no legitimate reason for delivering skelps, Ross-Gaul would unfailingly manage to create some pretext under which to punish a pupil, or preferably as many pupils as he could at the one time. Not just two for one: thirty-two for one if it could be achieved was one of Ross-Gaul's educational targets.

In class one morning, a pupil by the name of Edmund Stanley, a large boy for his age, let wind noisily whilst Ross-Gaul was in one of his rare teaching modes. Of course we all burst out laughing uncontrollably. Stanley was ordered to rise to his feet, which he did blushingly and his evident discomfiture contributed even more to our merriment. Ross-Gaul announced to Stanley that he would have to write one hundred lines (no, not the obvious "I must not fart in class") which ran: "Civilisation and courtesy require self-control." The rest of us continued to snigger, whereupon Ross-Gaul, sensing that there was more punitive mileage in this incident than had first met his eye, proceeded to enquire as to whom had been laughing the most or the loudest.

Informants rushed to name suspects and eventually the whole class managed to become implicated. Ross-Gaul, having almost instinctively managed to manufacture a situation where he could satisfy his need to make others miserable, with obvious relish ordered each and every one of us to write the same hundred lines as he had just dished out to Stanley moments before, thereby effectively ruining all our evening's play outdoors as the lines were required for the very next day. After class, Stanley got a good drubbing for getting us all into trouble, and we felt a little better for that.

Bullying was an institutionalised menace at Heriot's during the 1950s, with some masters providing the worst role models in that respect. Every class had its bullies, and they made life miserable for those of us who simply wanted to be left alone. Charles Bissett was a bully who was held in low esteem in spite of the fact that he was considered dangerous. He had a gang of henchmen who would do their best to terrorise anyone they fancied picking on. Bisset and his gang would play 'chariots', a game in which Bissett would be 'charioteer' and two henchmen would be 'horses'. Holding onto their blazer-tails, Bissett would drive his chariot straight into any unsuspecting boy in sight. On one occasion I was knocked heavily to the ground. As I got up to dust myself down, I noticed something hard and sharp in my mouth and spat it out: it was the best part of my new front tooth!

Mother immediately made an appointment for me at Mr McArthur's dental surgery, the first of many, as it was to turn out. Mr McArthur's sister acted as receptionist, and she bore a grave countenance indicative of the levels of fun one could expect at each visit. She would answer the telephone in sepulchral tones, uttering the less than reassuring words: "McArthur, Dentist." I am convinced that the television character Lurch's voice was modelled on hers. Once admitted to the surgery one was ushered into the waiting room where other glum-looking people sat until their turn for fun came.

Once in the chair I found that the best technique for dealing with the inevitable electrifying pain that invariably followed was to arch my back and grip the arms of the chair until my knuckles whitened. Mr McArthur never offered the luxury of any form of local anaesthetic currently available and the experience of having two holes drilled up either side of the nerve of my tooth stump was to say the least, aversive. Any brief respite from drilling would be followed by a blast of cold air that almost caused my vice-like grip on the chair to loosen as I shot up in the chair. A crown would then be glued onto the stump and I would be sent on my way. Within a day or two the crown would inevitably detach itself, usually ending up embedded in one of Nana's toffee apples, and the whole painful procedure would have to be redone over and over again. I came to hate the dentist almost as much as I hated Bissett for getting me into this situation. I heard a while ago that Bissett had died. Whether or not this is true I don't know, but in my opinion Death was too good for Bissett.

Another incident of bullying sticks in my mind, and on this occasion I was actively involved in a fisticuffs not of my own devising. My next-door neighbour in the class called Frank Scott had borrowed my eraser one morning and for some reason he wouldn't give it back to me when I asked him for it. An argument then ensued and, overhearing this, Bissett and his henchmen ruled that Frank and I would have to fight it out in the cycle sheds at lunchtime. We looked at one another in trepidation and tried unsuccessfully to convince the bullies that our disagreement didn't really warrant such a drastic solution, but their minds were already fixed on the prospect of a fight and word had already gone around the class to turn up at the cycle sheds at twelve o'clock to spectate.

As the midday bell rang to mark the appointed hour, Frank and I were escorted into the sheds where a makeshift ring was rapidly formed by a large number of boys who yelled at us, goading us to get going. Frank and I eyed one another, circling each other warily and looking for any sign of imminent attack, but none came from either reluctant adversary. After a few moments the bullies shouted that if we didn't get going then we would each have to fight them. I dimly heard someone shout: "Put your fists up!" and without pausing for further thought I instantly landed a punch on Frank's nose which exploded in a bloody mess. Frank was taken to the school lodge where the Janitor attended to his injury, whilst I was shouldered triumphantly round the playground as the victor. I've never felt so bad in my life, and that incident put me off physical violence for good. Frank, however, never seemed to hold it against me, and I like to think it was because he sensed that I was acting under duress and realised that had I paused for even a split second it would have certainly been my nose that became the casualty, rather than his. So that was a form of justice wrapped up within a grave injustice.

A rare treat for me for several years in Junior School was to be invited home to tea with a classmate Gerard Dott. Gerard was the son of Dr Eric Dott, the Paediatrician who years before had diagnosed that I was an anxious child, and I'm sure he recognised me. Mother was very pleased that I had shown the good taste to choose Gerard as a friend, and the fact that I had been invited into such an eminent family's home in Canaan Lane suggested to her that at last I had found my natural class position in society. The Dott family was like no other I had ever met. They always appeared calm, kind and considerate. Voices were never raised at any of the three boys, and the boys' behaviour did not appear to be under any form of control. Beowulf would be read after tea, and I found this a most civilising influence.

I took to the Dotts immediately, and when I returned home Mother was always keen to learn from me how the 'other half' lived. I was happy to regale her with, I admit, a somewhat embellished account of their liberalism and enlightened child-rearing philosophy, hoping that she might take a leaf out of their book or persuade Father to be less stern, although I did not need to embellish much. Whereas I called my parents Mummy and Daddy, Gerard's parents were known to their children as Eric and Sally. The only time I ever saw Sally remotely upset with us was when Gerard and I climbed onto the roof of one of the out-houses, proceeded to dismantle a chimney-stack and threw it onto the lawn. Gerard had told me that it would be OK to do this, and I taken him at his word. Sally appeared, evidently cross, but only said: "I'm vexed about this, boys." No hand or voice was raised, and the matter was never mentioned again. My own parents would have smacked me hard and sent me to bed without any supper, had they had a hand in chastisement for such an act of mindless vandalism.

Another lasting memory I have from that period is of my 'Uncle' Neil, who lived along the road in a second floor flat on the corner of Inverleith Row and Inverleith Terrace. He was not a blood relative;

rather a friend of Father's from the 1930s when they would ride their motorcycles to the Isle of Man to watch the TT races. They also shared a passion for photography and Neil was happy to accept Father's invitation to be Best Man at my parents' wedding in 1940.

Uncle Neil had been posted to Burma with the RAF and he suffered for the rest of his life. His fingernails had to be kept pared down to practically non-existence on account of what he referred to as 'jungle rot'. He had also contracted malaria and every year he would come down with an attack of 'the shivers', as he called them. Uncle Neil was an inventor, and his bachelor flat was crammed with gadgets such as lathes, stereo gramophones and various other pieces of technology, most of which he had designed and made himself.

One day Father said that Uncle Neil had built a television set and that we were going along the road to see it in the evening. I could scarcely contain my excitement because I had only just heard of television, and I bragged to my classmates that my Uncle had built a telly. Of course, no one believed me, but I said that I would tell them what I had seen on it the next day. That evening, we walked along the road to Uncle Neil's house. He proudly showed us a construction made out of Dexion, an open metal framework containing masses of wires, valves and a small circular cathode ray tube.

Ensuring that we were sitting comfortably, he switched it on and explained that we had to wait for it to warm up, which was what we had to do anyway for the radio in those days. The valves began to glow promisingly and eventually the cathode ray tube emitted an eerie green glow. After a few minutes Uncle Neil switched the apparatus off, saying how pleased he was that it all worked. When I asked him where the picture was, he informed me that there was no television transmission yet in Scotland and that it would be another two years before we could watch programmes. The following day my classmates quizzed me about what I had watched on TV the night before. "The screen", was my feeble reply, and my legendary reputation for veracity sank irredeemably from that moment. However, Uncle Neil lived to see his television set receiving the first signals in 1952, but he died shortly afterwards, his heart weakened by repeated attacks of malaria.

My last class in Junior School was with Gibbie Galloway in 12L. After Ross-Gaul, Galloway was a hugely civilising influence and he came across as being stern but fair. He was also popular with the boys and I did well academically in his year, being streamed into one of the top classes when I went up into the Senior School. My only recollection of being in 12L was when we all had to take the Eleven Plus examination in the Assembly Hall. Once again, it would be several decades before I recognised the test items that we had to complete. They were taken from the Weschler Intelligence Scale for Children, another psychological test I was to be taught to administer as a post-graduate Child Psychologist.

Going up into the 'big school' was a liberating experience for me as we had so many new subjects on the curriculum, including French, which I loved. We also had the very great privilege, although I am sure few of my contemporaries would agree with me here, of having an eccentric music teacher by the name of Dr Eric Smith. Dr

Smith's methods were, shall we say, somewhat unorthodox. One of his favourite techniques for encouraging projection of the voice was to insert the distal phalange of his thumb vertically between one's front teeth, to ensure that the mouth was opened sufficiently.

Because I had a decent ear and voice, I was fortunate to be chosen every year for the school choir, and some of my best school memories are of rehearsing for the Usher Hall annual school concert. For weeks we would learn off by heart arias and choruses by Handel and Purcell, each boy learning the treble, tenor or bass part, depending upon whose voice had broken or not. On their own, those parts made little sense or sound, but in the last weeks' run-up to the event itself we would be released from class to troop down to the Usher Hall itself where we would assemble behind the orchestra stall for final rehearsals. The sound that we produced filled me with awe, and when the whole piece came together properly I have to say it was most impressive.

Even today I remember all of the parts I learned over the years, from treble to bass, and I often try to sing along with arias from Judas Maccabeus such as 'Arm, Arm Ye Brave', or 'Let us now praise famous men', on my CD player. Alas, it soon became evident to me that Dr Smith had carefully rearranged and simplified the parts for our amateur voices, because the harmony I learned does not work other than for a few bars before becoming discordant. Eric Smith was, in my view, a genius, and quite underrated in the school, although I trust that his reputation extended beyond its gates. If I took only one thing away from Heriot's, it was my great love of classical music, and Eric Smith must take the credit for that.

As I progressed through the Senior school I was unfortunate to fall in with some bad company in the form of Ian Dunnett and another boy whose first name I can't recall because he liked to be known as 'Fritz', and who sported the newly fashionable crew cut hairstyle. Since we all lived within a stone's throw of one another on the North side of the city the three of us would meet up after school wearing green fisherman's knit pullovers by way of a uniform in which we thought we looked really cool. Ian's father was a Minister of the Church of Scotland whose manse in Summer Place was opposite the church. Ian was obsessed with firearms and anything to do with the military, as was Fritz. I was not particularly interested in any of this but found Dunnet's psychology fascinating. He would think nothing of catching a cat and torturing it; of firing his air rifle pellets through the stained glass windows of his father's church, and of creating explosive mixtures which he would either ignite in the public toilets in Trinity Park, or make into bombs which he would detonate beneath the goods trains carrying coal to Granton gasworks.

Dunnett and Fritz also habitually carried sheathed bayonets which they had 'obtained' from the school armoury and which they carried in sheaths beneath their long trousers. They were always on the lookout for trouble, and if there was none they soon enough generated it. One evening the three of us were walking along Summer Place a few doors along from the manse. Behind a pair of high gates the sound of someone washing his car could be heard. Dunnett kicked the gates aggressively as he went by, and the resident, showing his appreciation of Dunnett's actions, hosed him down for his trouble. Dunnett exploded with rage and demanded to see the person responsible for the soaking. A man appeared from within squirting more water at Dunnett. Almost in synchrony, Dunnett and Fritz drew their bayonets from beneath their clothes and proceeded to threaten the man, whom they pinned up against his wall, bayonet tips at his throat. The man turned white and begged to be left alone, whereupon Dunnett and Fritz seized his hose which they then cut up into a dozen or so small pieces.

Taking all of this casually in our stride, we then sauntered on into the park, only to be promptly arrested by the Police who had understandably been called. Instead of being taken directly to the Police Station we somehow managed to persuade the Police to speak with the Reverend Dunnett at the manse. After about half an hour the Police left and I cycled home, shaking as much as the victim of the crime. At assembly a couple of days later Mr Dewar announced that some items had gone missing from the school armoury, including two bayonets, but no mention of the Police incident was made. We heard no more about the matter and remarkably Dunnett and Fritz continued to attend the school.

My last experience with Dunnett, as if I hadn't learned my lesson already, was one day when we discovered that a door to the school roof had been left open in one of the turrets. We resolved to return to the school that evening to catch pigeons that we had seen outside. At about seven thirty we slunk into the quadrangle and climbed the stairs of one of the turrets. Our luck was in because the door was still unlocked. We proceeded out onto the roof and were happily chasing the pigeons around when we became aware of a commotion beneath us. Looking over the parapet we observed a cordon of Police Officers linking arms all the way round the entrance to the quadrangle. This was not the situation we had contrived to bring about.

Almost simultaneously we heard a familiar voice call out: "Come down!" We wasted no time in obeying the Headmaster's command, and we came upon him at the foot of the stairs backed up on either side by two huge plain clothes Police Detectives. How were we to know that he was interviewing parents in the room beneath us and that he had mistakenly thought that we were thieves attempting to steal lead from the roof? We went home in disgrace and the next day we were summoned to Dewar's study for six of the best, which in the event proved to be a mere tickle in comparison with Ross-Gaul's painful thrashings. I was convinced that expulsion would inevitably follow, and I faithfully promised Mr Dewar that I would have nothing further to do with Dunnett. Looking back with the knowledge of a Psychologist, I can confidently state that Dunnett was a textbook sociopath, but he was merely fascinating to me then.

Not that all the masters were themselves without their eccentricities. The Maths teacher would reduce us to helpless laughter as he announced that he was about to demonstrate a geometric proof, uttering the immortal words: "Just watch the board boys, whilst I run through it!" Some of the masters were fond of a drink. One of them, nicknamed 'Huck' McFee, together with a couple of other teachers, would regularly pay a lunchtime visit to the Greyfriar's Bobby Bar which they reached easily and unnoticed by slipping through Greyfriar's Churchyard from the school playground. There they would engage in liquid therapy before returning to their post-prandial classroom ordeals. One day, the Headmaster, on learning of this activity, strode out of the school in gown and mortar, stormed straight into the bar, and ordered the hapless dons back to school, much to the amusement of customers and to their eternal shame.

In the summer evenings after school, I would play outside with other children. When we moved from our tenement house in Canonmills to a maisonette in Warriston, I lost touch with my former pals in 'Puddocky'. However, I soon made new friends in Warriston, of whom most turned out to be Herioters as the school playing fields were on the doorstep. We would visit the wasteland at the South end of the street where a 'gang hut' was dug deep into the sandy soil and covered over with planks of wood and turves to camouflage it. Much smoking took place there but Miller homes now occupy this area, so that it only exists in my mind. Across the road, the derelict greenhouses that belonged to Duncan and Flockart, herbalists were also a favourite play area for a brief period and we had a literally smashing time there throwing stones at the panes of glass in the full knowledge that the site was to be developed by Millar the builders into residential homes situated on what was to become Warriston Drive, now a fifty year old residential estate.

Trips to the railway line at the back of Warriston Avenue were also made, with romantic episodes taking place in the covered guards vans once we became teenagers. Forays into Warriston Cemetery, in those days a beautiful tranquil place immaculately tended by a full time staff of gardeners, brought excitement when made in evenings during the winter months. It was a brave child indeed (and I was one of them) who would dare to venture into the vaults with a torch to see coffins stacked as high as the roof. The feeling of mounting fear bordering on terror as we went further and deeper into the crypts is unforgettable, such was the power of our childish imaginations.

The Red Lady's tomb was the jewel in the crown of the cemetery, and in those days was highly revered by all who visited the shrine. Visitors to the Cemetery today will be shocked at the state of the place. Whereas in the 1960s, full time labourers tended the graves, for over a decade 'upkeep' of the Cemetery was subcontracted to a private company which happily took the money but gave little in return other than neglect. The absence of the regular labourers gave out the message that no one really cared any more, and local malcontents soon found pleasure in wanton destruction.

Today, virtually nothing remains of that architectural treasure: a monument to the City Council's vandalism as well as that of a generation of Edinburgh louts. The photograph below, taken through the dark red glass which gave her her romantic name, shows the Red Lady asleep in her safe haven before she was rudely exposed to the elements, and today what little of her remains is a sad and sorry sight. A number of years ago, as my late Mother was taking a short cut through the cemetery, a Policeman advised her that it was not a safe place to be, a situation unimaginable in my day.

Little did I realise, when I took that innocent photograph, that one day the Red Lady would be no more, and that my careless snapshooting would be transformed into a piece of historical iconography. Had I done, I would have taken more care with the composition.

My latter years at Heriot's were not happy ones. Somehow the stuffing seemed to have been knocked out of me and I had stopped enjoying learning. Falling in with the wrong sort and too much institutionalised bullying had caused me to lose respect for many of the teachers, although Bert Jamie still stands out in my memory as a fine French and Russian master. Although I did not sit my leaving certificate examinations, I still retained sufficient French to pass at Higher level a decade later, so Mr Jamie's teaching must have been sound. Similarly, the English master 'Kipper' Heron gave me a love of Matthew Arnold and Shakespeare. But by the time I was sixteen I had had enough of school and after our Easter vacation in Innsbruck with Mr Walker the Art Teacher I did not return in the third term. The photos overleaf are of Bert Jamie and Kipper Heron respectively, pictures taken without either the knowledge or consent of either, I have to admit!

Rather than suffer the continuing humiliations of school, I would leave home at the usual hour dressed in my uniform and proceed to a local cafe in Goldenacre where I would smoke cigarettes, drink Coca Cola and play Buddy Holly and Eddie Cochrane records on the jukebox. In the afternoon I would walk though the Botanics, always timing my return home to coincide with school hours. This pretence went on for a week or so, until one day Father waved a letter at me that he had just received from the School, and enquired as to what I had been up to. When I told him, he seemed less upset than I had anticipated, but I suppose the thought of saving on school fees brought him some small compensation. My third childhood was now officially over and I was left with no prospects and with all the early promise gone. You could say that I was laughin' on the ither side o' ma face, and you wouldn't be wrong there.

CHAPTER 4

THE EARLY WORK YEARS

Since the age of around ten I had developed a fascination with photography. This was on account of Father being a keen amateur, and as a young child I had marvelled at the bits of photographic equipment lurking in various cupboards throughout the house. There was a folding camera, an exposure meter that Father had obtained in exchange for a quarter of a quarter of a pound of tea with a German in bombed out Hamburg, and there was a tripod. There were also boxes of unexposed glass plates (unexposed, that is, until I opened them in broad daylight!) and sheets of photographic paper with exotic-sounding names such as Agfa, Adox and Geveart.

Since I no longer had the chore of school attendance to put up with I set to work taking pictures with Father's ancient equipment, learning how to develop and print negatives in the attic with black-out curtains hung from the rafters and Father's home-made enlarger doing sterling service on a table. Dishes and chemicals were purchased and after a few weeks I was hooked. Unbeknown to me Father had been doing the rounds on the old boy network and had mentioned to a Solicitor friend of his that I had dropped out of school, was only interested in photography and that he despaired of me.

As luck would have it, the Solicitor was a personal friend of Alan Harper, the Managing Director of J Campbell Harper Photographers, which had just recently moved premises to Dundas Street. Mr Harper kindly offered to take me on as a photographic apprentice, and in 1959 I began work there at £2.00 gross per week, where I joined Ian Nicol, another apprentice photographer, in the darkrooms in the basement. From the start, I was in my element, and with fatherly encouragement from Marion Boron the Manager, I flourished. In the fallow winter months we were unlucky if we got get one film per day to process, leaving plenty of time for experimentation. Marion insisted that all apprentices should become members of the Edinburgh Photographic Society, and every fourth Wednesday night we would attend a talk or have our monthly exhibition pictures subjected to the stern criticism of our betters.

With every darkroom facility available at work, I soon became proficient at producing big enlargements which I entered into the Beginners' section of the EPS. Such social recognition meant a lot to me then, and it more than compensated for my failure to make anything of school after the age of eleven. In spite of being paid a pittance even by the then standards of the day, it was an utter delight to do the only thing I wanted to do and I would have worked for nothing if truth were told.

Over the months I managed to save up enough money to buy a decent modern camera. Armed with it, I would explore the city and its environs, snapping away morning, noon and night. I would experiment with very fine grain emulsions and also with very high speed ones. Good shots were enlarged and mounted to be entered into the monthly photo judgings at the EPS. By the end of the first year I had received the President's Trophy for the best print in the Beginners' Section; a silver medal which hangs in a frame over my desk today.

My camera and I would spend many evenings in the Botanics looking for good compositions, or go up town after dark to experiment with the fastest emulsions of the day. Examples of the sort of photography I engaged in then can be seen overleaf. The picture in the Botanics was taken on Panatomic-X, a fine-grained film and the one of the Monseigneur Cinema in Princes street was taken on Royal X Pan, the fastest emulsion available at the time. The picture of East Arthur Place shows its demolition in the early 1960s. Although the composition was chosen for its pictorial value, it may be appreciated today as a piece of social history and it gives a flavour of times long gone when children played happily in the streets unsupervised.

Evening read—Royal Botanic Garden

Princes Street—1960

East Arthur Place—1961

Having even a small income gave me greater social mobility, and I struck up a friendship with another Campbell Harper employee, Jack Galbraith, who was employed as a Sales Assistant at Campbell Harper's retail outlet in South St David's Street where Dave Pearson was the Manager. Every day my job was to mount my bicycle and pedal up Dundas Street and along George Street to the shop to collect customers' films for developing and printing. In the summer, Ian Nicol, the other apprentice, and I had our work cut out as almost one hundred films would be awaiting collection, processing and delivery of prints the following day. Campbell Harper's were committed to a twenty-four hour service and it was our job to see that they lived up to their reputation.

My daily visits to the shop involved exchanging banter with Jack and we soon became friends as he lived at Pilton not far from my home. Jack was what one would now call a 'flash dude' if ever there was one, and he combined a 'hard man' exterior with a natural easy charm and wit. He dressed immaculately in a Burton's suit and sheepskin jacket and drove a powder blue Ford Consul Mark II which he had 'souped up' as any self-respecting young motorist of the day would do. This made the car quite nimble (it could reach 30mph in first gear) and the exhaust note was stunning, particularly on the overrun when it would give off a delicious burbling sound. That car was a totty magnet if ever there was one, and consequently Jack had countless girlfriends. However, he was also a man's man and with his Policeman friend Corrie the three of us would enjoy nights up town in the various cafes and bars surrounding Princes Street.

My main ambition at that time was to become a motorist like Jack, and to that end I managed to save up the princely sum of twenty-five pounds which I immediately exchanged for a Morris Eight Series Two advertised at Jock's Lodge Motors. My Father had advised me on the Morris because it possessed hydraulic brakes and an SU carburettor, which were considered to be superior to Austin cars, which had cable brakes and a Zenith carburettor. Father taught me to drive in about three weeks by allowing me to take the wheel from home to Dundas Street where he would then take the wheel, leaving me at my workplace whilst he drove on to his office in Charlotte Square. In the evening he would drive to Dundas Street to pick me up and I would drive us both home.

My driving test took place at Portobello, which my Father had already identified as the most likely venue, and he made sure that I was well acquainted with the area. Only one eventful incident occurred during the test that led me to believe that I had failed. The Examiner was a very large man and he could barely fit into the small front seat of the Morris. When it came to do the hill start, I increased the revs, let in the clutch and released the handbrake. The car stood perfectly still whilst acrid smoke wafted up from beneath the floorboards. I explained that the clutch wasn't up to a hill start with such a heavy load and asked the Examiner if he might get out so that I could complete the exercise. He informed that this would be illegal, so I carried on with the test with sinking heart. At the end I was told that because I had not let the car slip backwards on the hill, I had technically passed!

With wheels I felt free for the first time in my life and Jack and I would take our cars out for rides and generally show off to anyone who might notice us, girls in particular. But my Morris Eight was of the anorak variety and Jack had better success in that department with his American-styled Ford Consul than I had. However, along with Corrie, when he was not on late shift, the three of us would roam the city and its environs, often going for a long run at the weekend down to places such as North Berwick and Cove Bay for a bit of amateur photography.

After a few months the Morris began to show its age: twenty-five years to be precise. My efforts at elementary 'tuning' had paid off on the one hand, but on the other was the inevitable strain put on the engine which I had taken out, stripped down, refurbished and reassembled. An obstinate oil leak subsequently proved impossible to fix and I sold it. What I really hankered for was an Austin Seven and as luck would have it one turned up in Alexander's Garage in Pitt Street. It had been laid up for many years and someone had removed the sunroof. Nonetheless, it started after a bit of fettling and I was informed that I could have it for four pounds, just two weeks' wages. A couple of pounds paid for an aluminium sheet to cover the roof and within a few days it became my daily means of transport.

In those days MoT certificates had just become mandatory, and I was apprehensive of the Austin ever passing on account of the notoriously poor brakes. But as luck would have it, I had found, through a neighbour, part-time evening work that involved preparing car bodies for respraying. Our Saturday advertisement in the Edinburgh

Evening news carried the promise: 'Your car resprayed from £30.' Jimmy Simpson, one of the mechanics who did occasional work for us, issued an MOT certificate over the 'phone based on my optimistic description of its stopping power, and that little vehicle served me on a daily basis for two years.

The Austin Seven was probably the most reliable car I'd ever owned, and home repairs were childishly simple to undertake. In the depths of an Edinburgh winter it would unfailingly start after a couple of swings on the starting handle, and where other modern vehicles would fail to ascend Dundas Street on account of a fresh fall of snow, my little Austin would purr faultlessly up the hill. On one such occasion, when Wolseleys, Singers and Hillmans were lying abandoned at the roadside, I sped by to the cheers of nearby road workers. So fond did I become of Austin Sevens that I purchased one a couple of years ago but had to pay six thousand pounds for it! With hindsight, I should never have sold any of my good old cars.

When Jack became twenty-one he expressed the wish to buy a motorcycle as he had been a keen biker before he bought the Consul. Across the road from Campbell Harper's in Dundas Street was a firm called L H King, which supplied second-hand bikes, and after trying out a few Jack settled for a 250cc BSA. On the following day he said that he would come round to my house so that we could both have a ride along the Barnton straight where you could really open up the throttle. He said that he would be round at seven o'clock and as it was a beautiful sunny evening I looked forward to the thrills of motorcycling as I'd never been on a bike before.

At seven fifteen there was still no sign of Jack: unusual because he used to be ever so punctual. At eight-twenty the 'phone rang. It was Corrie telling me that Jack had been killed outright when his bike had veered across the road sending him under a Corporation bus just a few yards from his house on his way to mine. In those days there were no compulsory crash helmets and Jack's head had gone under a wheel. I was spared the identification of Jack's body that Corrie undertook, being the first to hear of the accident as he was on Police duty at the time. The only mercy was that we both hadn't been on the bike, but that was a small consolation. To say that we were all devastated is an understatement. For weeks afterwards I went about as if in a daze, and at Jack's funeral many young women whom none of us had ever met before openly wept and wailed.

The pictures above show Jack on the left and me on the right larking about in the photographic studio at Campbell Harper's a few weeks before his death. The loss of Jack's life was to jolt all of us out of our happy-go-lucky existences and put a smile on the other side of our faces for a very long time.

But life had to go on although my ties with Campbell Harper felt as if they were loosening, partly on account of Jack's absence from the shop which never felt the same again, and partly because I somehow sensed that there was no future for me there. I began to seek more remunerative employment and one night I spotted an advertisement in the Evening News for a Photographer at the Scottish Central Library in the Lawnmarket. I applied, was interviewed and was offered the post at a wage of £7.10/- per week: more than three times what I was being paid at Campbell Harper's.

My main office/studio was a vast room on the top floor, some five stories up, with a huge darkroom behind it. The sole camera was a large device fixed to the floor which held a cartridge of thirty-five millimetre film. Documents for photographing were placed beneath a glass platen and operation of a footswitch clicked the camera shutter and moved the film onto the next frame. The previous incumbent of the post had managed to arrange the work so that it took only one or two hours of the day, leaving him free to do the Express newspaper crossword with the aid of the Janitor who inhabited a small office on the ground floor at the font of the building.

The Chief Librarian was known as 'Faither' by the Janitor, who had apparently been his batman when they were both in the Royal Navy.

Faither was never seen sober. He would arrive at work at around ten o'clock to sign a few letters until twelve when it was time to top up the alcohol levels at Deacon Brodie's across the road. By three o'clock Faither was so intoxicated that when he arrived back in the building the Janitor often had to call a taxi to ferry him back home to North Berwick. The Police next door were always very helpful in ensuring that Faither's battered Hillman Minx did not receive a parking ticket as he usually just dumped it outside the door at a jaunty angle to the kerb. I distinctly recall Faither ringing me up one day on the internal telephone, asking me to discuss some urgent matter with him in his office, only to find him slumped unconscious over his desk by the time I arrived one minute later!

Because of the amount of spare time available at work, and my own research shows that in spite of this I trebled the output of the Photographic Department in the two years I worked there, much time was available for reading. One of the bonuses of working in an interlending library was that it was filled with books on every conceivable subject, and I would often browse among the shelves in the upper regions of the building. I came across a section on Psychology and began to read my way through the Collected Works of Sigmund Freud as well as those of Carl Jung. Of course, I understood little of what I read having had no training in critical thinking, but one day I happened upon a copy of the Stanford Binet Intelligence Test. Browsing through it I recognised some items that had been administered at school and, as a copy of the whole test was included, I self-administered it and scored it up. I came out as Superior Adult Three, which I thought was not bad.

After two years I tired of the repetitiousness of photographing dusty and frankly dismal documents such as 'The Paisley Pamphlets' or the 'Ayrshire Gazette' for the years 1886-1900 inclusive, and I sorely missed what I considered to be 'proper' photography. One evening I saw an advertisement in the Evening News for a Medical Photographer at the Princess Margaret Rose Orthopaedic Hospital at Fairmilehead, and as I had acquired a new girlfriend and knew that things were serious between us, I felt that I needed to improve my career prospects as well as my earnings. In spite of knowing nothing whatsoever about medical photography, and possessing no formal qualifications as there were none to be had in those days, I was short-listed and invited to attend an interview. There were three other candidates who looked much more mature than I did, but I clutched onto my portfolio of exhibition prints made for the Edinburgh Photographic Society by way of reassuring myself, all the while hoping to persuade others that I was a photographer to be taken seriously.

After waiting for what seemed an interminable time, I was invited to enter a room with a large table around which were seated about eight consultant orthopaedic surgeons. They put me at my ease and began to ask a number of medical questions to which I had absolutely no answers. As each eminent surgeon put to me yet another impossible question, I began to feel that the interview was about to be terminated. However, one of the people round the table introduced himself as Mr Whitley, Chief Medical Photographer at the Royal National Orthopaedic Hospital in London, and he enquired as to what I had brought with me. I took out some prints from my portfolio over which he enthused before passing them round the table. Two of the consultants asked if they could have framed copies and Mr Whitley gave me a knowing look.

Having thus concentrated the minds of the surgeons on matters photographic and my abilities in that department, I was then quizzed about the names of various bones in the body. Remembering my childhood interest in anatomy, I was able to acquit myself well on this subject, and faces visibly brightened round the table. Everybody thanked me for bringing the pictures and I was asked to wait outside for a decision to be made. After a few minutes, the Professor of Orthopaedic Surgery invited me back into the room where I was informed that I had been successful in my application, but because I had no specific experience in medical photography, I was to be attached to Mr Whitley's unit in London for a period of three months training. I accepted without a second thought and two weeks later I boarded the London train, saying *au revoir* to my new found girl-friend and *bonjour* to a new-found loneliness in digs in London.

Arriving at King's Cross station at about nine o'clock at night, I set out to look for accommodation. Somehow it had never occurred to me that I should have made arrangements before leaving Edinburgh, but I alighted from the train and set out across the Euston Road. I found a street called Argyll Square, the same name as that of my girl friend Elizabeth's digs in Portobello. Some of the properties had notices in the window advertising vacancies, so I rang a doorbell and waited with anticipation. A scruffy looking woman answered and asked what I wanted. I said that I needed a room, and she asked me for how long. "Three months", I replied. Her faced took on a strange expression, but she nonetheless invited me in and proceeded to escort me up two flights of stairs to a room for which she was asking three pounds per week bed and breakfast.

I put a shilling in the meter and lit the gas fire; one uncannily resembling the one that Mr Murray had had in Edinburgh for which spares had been allegedly obsolete for two decades! I surveyed the room as I warmed myself. The window didn't close properly and the bedclothes were damp and musty. Ten minutes later, the gas went out and another shilling had to be fed into the meter. After five shillings' worth I decided to hit the sack. Exhausted, I opened my case, unpacked my pyjamas and went to sleep. I was awakened shortly after by the sound of people shouting on the landing outside. Harsh words were exchanged which made Michaelina's language sound refined. Women's screams were uttered and feet clattered up and down the stairs for most of the night.

In the morning I went downstairs for breakfast. A dingy basement room was filled with cigarette smoke and the smell of fat frying. A number of burly individuals who looked like truck-drivers sat around eating greasy fry-ups and drinking tea from enormous mugs. I ate what I could myself, then left for work, which was a mere fifteen minutes' walk along the Euston Road to Great Portland Street where the Institute of Orthopaedics was situated: not a bad commuting time for London. The staff there made me very welcome and enquired as to where I might be staying. When I told them, they were horrified, and said that I would have to get out of there as soon as possible. I was tactfully informed that I had been sleeping in a brothel! Fortunately, a member of staff allowed me to stay at her house until I found more suitable accommodation out at Stanmore, the location of the Royal

National Orthopaedic Hospital where Mr Whitley ran another photographic department. After Argyll Square, I felt in heaven as I looked out of the window and spied an English apple orchard. My wheel of life had thus come full circle.

My three months in London dragged as I could not afford to return regularly to Edinburgh to be with my future wife Elizabeth. At the weekend I would take a Northern Line train from Stanmore to King's Cross and walk around the city. But my heart wasn't really in it and I would return home to my digs to play the guitar. Fortunately, I was a big fan of Bob Dylan and I learned to play most of his popular numbers, much to the appreciation of my landlady, I'm sure. One weekend Elizabeth came down from Edinburgh and we went into Bravington's Jewellers at King's Cross to purchase engagement rings. We looked at one another with some misgiving as we sat on the underground train, but deep down I felt that my life was definitely changing for the better and the future looked promising for the first time in a long time.

Having landed the job at PMR I now felt financially secure enough to be able to marry Elizabeth; after all, a Medical Photographer's salary was as good as a Teacher's one, so no shame in that. Our wedding took place at Elizabeth's Father's kirk in Portlethen, Kincardineshire. Corrie was Best Man and Ian Nicol from Campbell Harper's was our official photographer. In anticipation, we had purchased a flat in Comiston Road for £1,600 after having managed to save the requisite £400 deposit, which in those days was the sum required. No chance of lending to folk that couldn't pay back the loan. Bankers were responsible in those days, and so were we. Although we could have lived together in the flat before we got married whilst we were doing it up, we lived apart until we were wed: all part of good old Morningside respectability.

After the wedding we travelled back from Aberdeen in an Alvis car that my Father had owned before he sold it to Ian Nicol. My Father had paid £80 for the car and after a year or two he sold it to Ian for £25. After running it for some time Ian then sold it to me for £5. Once Ian had taken our wedding photographs I printed them to help pay for our new found independence. On the way back from Aberdeen with all the wedding presents in the boot and the back of the car, a big end went. Although the car was still running, it was clear that its demise was imminent. I telephoned Father who told me to stay where we were in Glenfarg and that he would drive up to meet us.

Once all of the wedding presents had been transferred to his car, the problem was what to do with the crippled Alvis? Father and I debated the issue and came up with a brilliant solution: remove the number plates and drive it over the lay-by into the gorge below. So I started the engine, selected fist gear and pushed the accelerator pedal. The car moved towards the edge of the layby and at the last moment I opened the door and jumped out, leaving the car to carry on into thin air, landing with a crash in the burn below.

The next morning, as my new wife and I were enjoying a Sunday morning lie-in, the telephone rang. I answered, expecting the salutations of a well-wisher. The voice at the other end said, "This is the Perthshire Constabulary. We have reason to believe that you are the owner of an abandoned vehicle and we wish to interview you immediately". I rang Corrie, Best Man and Police Constable, to ask for his advice. Corrie said that we had to go to Glenfarg right away and sort things out. On arrival at the Police Station it was evident that the local Constabulary were unimpressed by our contempt, not only for the scenic beauty of the glen, but also for its inhabitants. Unbeknown to us, a local vagrant had been living in a modest wooden dwelling just below the lay-by. Enjoying the habitual serenity of the burnside, his peace had been shattered by the passage overhead of a motor vehicle with lights blazing, which had crashed into the burn.

Fearing that a fatal accident might have ocurred as the glen was a notorious accident spot, the tramp had immediately walked to the nearest point of civilisation and made an emergency telephone call to the authorities. The Police, aware of the dangerous nature of the twisting road through the glen, had spent the whole night searching the burn, probing the waters for bodies. When we arrived in Glenfarg the following day, the Police were consequently not in the best of moods to entertain our account of events. But Corrie came into his own: his finest hour, in my opinion. Immediately bonding with a fellow Police Officer, he put our case impeccably: the care-free newly weds; himself their Best Man just the day before; the glowing character references; the admittedly foolish, panicked decision that was very much regretted by the perpetrator in the cold light of day, etc, etc.

The upshot was that the Police gave me twenty-four hours to remove the wreck on pain of being fined under the Litter Act, the only legislation that they could charge me under. I contacted the nearest garage a few miles away and they undertook to winch the vehicle out of the ravine if in exchange they could take ownership of the wreck. I immediately agreed. Today, such a vehicle, even in wrecked condition, could fetch several thousands of pounds. But what puzzled me about the whole affair was how the Police had managed to link the vehicle to me: after all, I had removed the number plates before ditching it. One must not readily dismiss the powers of forensic research. In the glove compartment lay a receipt for servicing made out to my Father years before. On discovering this, the Police had telephoned him, whereupon he readily admitted that he had owned the vehicle some years ago and had sold it to one named Ian Nicol.

Further Police research eventually revealed that Ian had sold it to me, and the paper trail was thereby complete. From marital bliss the night before to fear of imprisonment the next day: well, laughin' on the ither side o' ma face doesn't do justice to the seriousness of the situation. Looking back, I honestly believe that I was a whisker away from a jail sentence for manslaughter had that tramp been killed.

When I returned from London to take up my post at the hospital in Edinburgh I found that my photographic studio and darkroom were still in the process of becoming as the new clinical research unit building was somewhat behind schedule. All the photographic apparatus that had been ordered was sitting in an empty office and I set about unpacking it and familiarising myself with what were to be the new tools of my trade. Soon enough the building was completed and one of my first tasks was to act as official photographer at the opening ceremony attended by Her Royal Highness Princess Margaret Rose, after whom the hospital had been named in 1933. The photograph below shows Professor J I P James, Chair of Orthopaedics with Her Royal Highness and one of the young patients.

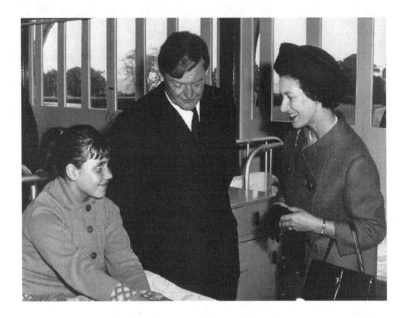

Work soon got under way and I was fortunate to acquire a photographic assistant by the name of Mike Devlin, who had been an apprentice at David Yerbury's studio. Between us we provided what I recall to be an excellent and highly professional photographic service to ten consultant surgeons, whilst being able to have plenty of fun at the same time. One event that stands out in my memory was the annual pantomime, which I ended up directing as well as participating in. I suppose I had Mother to thank for such thespian tendencies. One highlight was a gentle lampoon of some of the more colourful consultants to the tune of 'Lily the Pink', which had in timely fashion reached number one in the hit parade on the very week of the pantomime: such prescience!

Working at the hospital, Mike and I got to know one of the patients, Keith Burrows, below, who was to go on to become a maths graduate and one of the first commercial computer programmers in the UK. Keith was an avid chess-player and accomplished blues guitarist. He suffered from a congenital condition known as Albright's Syndrome, which meant that his long bones were unstable and liable to fracture at any moment; even a fit of coughing could result in Keith fracturing several ribs. Keith was also interested in photography, and every day he would wheel himself along to the photographic studio from the nearby ward to entertain us on the guitar, whilst chatting about photography. Once he was discharged he would return to his workplace at IBM in Manchester, where he continued to work until his disabilities became too much for him to cope with.

Keith and I developed a lifelong friendship, although Keith's life was regrettably to turn out to be significantly shorter than my own. I often think that if I had not met him I might never have become a Psychologist, as one of his ways of coping with severe disability was to engage in black humour. One of his favourite sayings, when hospitalised again for a few months after yet another fracture, was: "Oh well, as one door shuts, so another closes!" Another was a parody of one of The Bachelors' songs that went: "I believe for every drop of rain that falls a flower grows", which Keith rendered into: "I believe for every drop of rain that falls someone gets wet".

Keith would also relish relating his many brushes with the hospital authorities since he knew his rights and always used impeccable logic to support his case. On one particularly long bout of hospitalisation he asked the Ward Sister if he could have his work computer brought in so that he could do some programming, as he was bored just lying in bed all day and had all his faculties. His request was declined, so Keith penned a letter to Matron repeating his request. On the following day Matron came to his bedside in person to inform him that his request had again been refused. When Keith asked her to justify her decision she said that no other patient had a computer and that hospital policy was that all patients had to be treated in exactly the same way. Keith then pointed out to her that the patient in the bed on his left had a plaster on his right leg and the patient on his right had a plaster on his left arm. Keith demanded Matron's compliance with her own policy and that he be treated exactly the same as other patients, insisting that his right leg and left arm be put in plaster. Keith got his computer!

One evening whilst sitting drinking in the Cafe Royal, Keith and I became aware that someone at the next table was staring at him. As if through mutual telepathy, I hoisted Keith onto my knee and stuck my hand up the back of his jacket, whereupon Keith uttered the immortal ventriloquist's dummy line: "A gottle of geer!". That soon had the observer laughin' on the ither side o' his face and the spontaneity as well as the success of that ploy stayed with us both for many years after. Keith was to die in his sleep of choking whilst drunk, aged thirty-three years. At his funeral, attended by just short of two hundred people, his mates had a beautiful wreath made up with the words "Sadly Missed" written in flowers, with the 'M' crossed out and replaced by a 'P'.

Early married life was busy but also novel and challenging. Each morning Elizabeth would leave the house to teach at St Serf's School for Girls, whilst I left to go to the hospital. With two decent incomes we were now able to enjoy a bit of local socialising. Every Friday night we would meet up with friends and workmates at Milnes Bar in Hanover Street. In those days Milne's was known as 'The Little Kremlin' on account of the Socialists and Communists who frequented it. Leading lights to be encountered there on a regular basis were the likes of Hugh Mc Diarmid, Robert Garioch, Edwin Morgan, Ian Crichton Smith, Norman McCaig, George Mackay Brown, Sorley McLean and Sydney Goodsir Smith. Sandy Moffat, an art college undergraduate of the day and friend of a friend, painted an imaginary gathering in Milne's of all of those literary giants. The picture now hangs in the National Galleries of Scotland and I chose it for the cover because it captures brilliantly the atmosphere of the day. Only the thick cloud of fag smoke is missing!

After four or five years at the hospital I began to feel that photography was not stretching me any more; the challenges had been overcome and the work began to take on a repetitive character with few new technical problems presenting themselves or opportunities for creativity arising. I also noticed that I was becoming more interested in the patients themselves than the job of photographing them. One thing that repeatedly struck me was how one patient with a relatively minor deformity or disability would treat the whole episode as a great catastrophe, whereas another, born horribly crippled, would make relatively light of things. My instincts as an amateur psychologist were beginning to show, and I began to undertake some further reading on the subject from where I had left off when employed at the Library.

One day my Mother had an accident at home. She slipped on a wet step and fractured her heel. After a few weeks in plaster she attended the Princess Margaret Rose Hospital as an outpatient, where Professor James examined her. Noticing her name, and no doubt her physical resemblance to me, he enquired if she was any relation. "I'm his Mother," she replied. "Then tell him he's wasted here!" said the Professor. Mother duly relayed his comments to me, and this gave me the confidence to commence academic study once again, this time at evening classes where I gained O levels in English, Mathematics and Biology. I then did what on looking back appears positively reckless: I left my job to become a full time day student at Napier College (now Napier University), where I gained sufficient 'Highers' to be admitted to Edinburgh University to read for an Honours degree in Psychology. Things were hard financially for the first year as I only qualified for a Local Authority grant of £500 for a whole year.

At Edinburgh University I flourished. No more beatings, no more lines, fascinating subjects such as Metaphysics and Psychology, and a State grant equivalent to my very reasonable salary at the hospital. In the summer vacations I worked as a Ward Orderly at the Astley Ainslie Hospital in Canaan Lane where I earned even more money. At Christmas I drove a GPO van through the night on a twelve-hour shift that paid double time, and I had soon saved enough money to buy a second hand car which lasted the family five years. No such possibilities for today's mature students, I'm afraid.

Summer jobs were always an experience. At the Astley Ainslie I was employed as a Ward Orderly at the phenomenal rate of £30 per week, more than I had been paid as a Medical Photographer. I worked alternate weeks on two male rehabilitation wards, one designated for smokers, the other for non-smokers. My first job of the day was to empty the sputum cups that sat on patients' bedside cabinets. On the smoking ward they would invariably be full of disgusting yellow-brown liquid. On the non-smoking ward they were invariably unused. I immediately stopped smoking on the basis of this incontrovertible evidence.

Sometimes a situation would arise that required a bit of lateral thinking. One example that stands out in my memory involved a patient who was recovering from a colostomy operation. One of my jobs was to assist him change his plastic bag which was situated on the abdominal wall. One evening, just before visiting time, he buzzed for assistance. I drew the screens, pulled down his pyjamas and was met with the sight of a bag inflated to bursting point with gas. At that moment Sister entered the ward to tell us to draw all screens back as the visitors were coming. There was no time to change the bag so I hit upon the bright idea of taking off my name badge and using the pin to puncture it, thereby successfully deflated it. But I had failed to think this through and as a cloud of noxious gas filled the ward Sister was heard to shout: "Mr Dodds! What's going on here?" Too late, aerosols of fragrances were rushed in to quench the stench, and I was as popular as a fart in a space suit that day, or indeed a fart in a colostomy bag for that matter.

Another summer vacation job presented itself one year, when the twenty year-old mystery of Dandy and the chicken was to be fortuitously resolved: too late for my Grandfather, I'm afraid. Next door to their house was the tied cottage of Mr Hamilton, the Waterman, as he was known to my Grandfather. Mr Hamilton was an Inspector at the Liberton Filtration Plant, a vast Victorian site concealed from the public by trees and steep grassy banks, where the water that travels forty miles underground from Talla reservoir is filtered before being distributed to the population of Edinburgh. Hearing that I was looking for a summer vacation job, he had put in a good word for me and for two summers I worked there cutting the acres of grassy bank with an Allen scythe, or hoeing hundreds of yards of gravel paths to keep them free from weeds. Another student shared the work with me and the picture below shows us both in front of one of the Greek 'temples' that concealed the Victorian waterworks' machinery.

The Foreman of the gang of labourers was a short, stocky and surly bloke called Fred, who enjoyed making our student lives miserable and who took pleasure in watching us out in the pouring rain whilst he sat in the hut drinking tea. We put up with Fred for a whole summer, but when our vacation came to an end we decided to let him know what we really thought of him by nailing his work boots to the floor of his locker.

By complete contrast was Willie Duncan, a former labourer in his seventies who came out of retirement every summer to scythe the grassy banks that were too steep for the Allen scythe to be risked on. 'Willie the Scythe' was a true Edinburgh Worthy, and he had many tales to tell. One was when a young labourer had turned up the worse for wear the morning after a session at his local. Willie saw that the lad was incapable of work and so he told him to lie down inside one of the huge steel pipes that lay around the works. Willie heaped some straw over the end of the pipe whilst the lad slept it off for a few hours undetected. Of course, Fred asked where the lad was at break time, but Willie covered for him, saying that he was working overtime at a distant part of the site where no one ever went! As The Bard said, "The man's the gowd for a' that".

The picture above shows Willie in full scytheman's outfit. The muscles in his arm are a sight to behold and I have no doubt that few seventy year olds could work eight hours a day flat out with only a half hour break for lunch and two ten minute breaks for a fag. There is no corresponding picture of Fred, for obvious reasons.

EPILOGUE

That was to be my last year as a young or not so young adult in Edinburgh. I had come to realise that the fun times were over and that I had grown up, in spite of myself. In 1974 I graduated *summa cum laude* in Psychology from Edinburgh University. I was then accepted to a post-graduate course in Child Development at Nottingham University where I stayed on to obtain a Doctorate, graduating PhD in 1980. I eventually became Director of a research unit in their Department of Psychology. During my twenty years there I published over fifty scientific papers and three textbooks on rehabilitation. In 1996 I left academia to become a Clinician and to undertake Expert Witness work at the Royal Courts of Justice in London. I am now a semi-retired Consultant Neuropsychologist working in Nottingham with brain-injured adults and autistic children. I have a son, a daughter and three grandchildren.

But Edinburgh remains my Alma Mater, and I return to the city as often as I can, now as a visitor rather than an inhabitant. Right now I'm standing at the mouth of Warriston Crescent, looking down with Tanfield behind me. Why, there's Marjerie tucking her skirt up into her knickers so she can skip on the rope that the Johnson sisters are swinging. Someone's asking me if I want to play peevers. "Nae fear, I'm no' a cissy", I retort. Stuart Harrod's already halfway up a tree beckoning me to join him. And there's Arnold Kemp with a new bike that he's not letting me have a go on, toerag that I am. I'd better not tell him he's going to die long before I do, but I'm tempted. At that moment Michaelina pokes her head up from the basement at Number Four. "Ye dirty wee bugger!" she shouts at me, as I watch the Store milk horse lift its tail to drop a stinking pile on the cobbles. That'll keep the scaffies busy tomorrow. And you should see the look of disbelief on Christina Kemp's face when I tell her that I'm going to be a Writer just like her father. Then, as quickly as they appeared, they're gone, and as their voices die away I catch myself laughin, and not for the first time, on the ither side o' ma face.